Confessions of a
KAMIKAZE
COWBOY

Confessions of a

KAMIKAZE
COWBOY

BY

DIRK BENEDICT

Introduction by William Dufty
Author of SUGAR BLUES

NEWCASTLE PUBLISHING CO., INC.
North Hollywood, California
1987

Edited by Hank Stine
Cover photograph by Greg Gorman

FIRST EDITION

A NEWCASTLE BOOK
First Printing, April 1987
9 8 7 6 5 4 3 2
Printed in the United States of America

This book is dedicated to:

Desi Arnaz
Count Basie (William)
Ingrid Bergman
Humphrey Bogart
Ray Bolger
Yul Brynner
Nat King Cole
Michael Conrad
Gary Cooper
Scatman Crothers
Duke Ellington
Joan Hackett
Jere Hudson
Ted Knight
Andy Kaufman
Alan Ludden
Steve McQueen
Agnes Moorehead
Ozzie Nelson
Marlin Perkins
Donna Reed
Simone Signoret
Jacqueline Susann
Francois Truffaut
Forrest Tucker
John Wayne
Keenan Wynn
Efrem Zimbalist Senior

CONTENTS

INTRODUCTION

Way back in the Stone Age, when jazz was a verb and cocaine was called snow, and you could buy it at your corner
drugstore over the counter like aspirin, things you couldn't
buy there—except maybe under the counter—were sold on
street corners by dirty old men and called raincoats, or rub-
bers. The only kind of population control not considered im-
moral or illegal was World War I.

Way back then when Great Grandma was a groupie, there
was this little Latin guy with patent-leather hair who called
himself Rudolph Valentino. He was a helluva dancer and he
used to toss his pelvis around doing a naughty dance created
by some macho Argentine pimps. They called it the tango.

The tango epidemic became a subject of convulsive moral
controversy. Bigtown vice squads used to raid dance halls and
carry off tango dancers in horse-drawn paddy wagons. The
Pope denounced it as a "hypocritical excuse for things too
shameful to discuss." There were clamorous voices calling
for its prohibition. Naturally, with this kind of megamarket-
ing, it became very, very popular. Girls like Great Grandma
used to practice it in secret behind locked bedroom doors.
And when they saw Valentino do it in the movies, they got
very, very excited. The old girls never told you about this?
Well, then, allow me.

In Chicago there was a little Polish girl, a high-school
dropout who dreamed of becoming an opera star. Opera was
like MTV, only louder and longer and live. Movie stars and
microphones hadn't been invented yet; the big international
celebrities were hefty ladies who could rattle the rafters at the
Met for hours at a time. The little girl from Chicago couldn't

cut it, everything went amiss for her and she ended up as a star of silent pictures. One of the first. Her name was Gloria Swanson. She used to hang out with Valentino in Hollywood. They rode horseback together and danced the tango in the Hollywood hills. They were both in their early twenties —filthy rich and plenty famous. They had the world by the tail.

One day Rudy had a pain in his pelvis. At first, they thought it was from overwork. They took him to the hospital, where the doctors wanted to operate. Don't they always? Rudy never got out of that hospital alive. His funeral, of course, was a riot. Gloria knew it would be, so she refused to go. She hated funerals. And hospitals. And operations. Unlike the ladies in black veils you've read about who hung out around his tomb, Gloria always remembered Rudy in her own very private way.

She became famous in Hollywood, among those who knew her, for trying to talk people out of having unnecessary operations. Especially attractive young men. And especially in the pelvis. It was her way of remembering Rudy.

As a dropout, Gloria read every book on health she could lay her hands on. She was not impressed by famous surgeons in white coats with diplomas on their walls. Butchers wear white coats too, she used to say. One doctor who did impress her charged two dollars a visit for telling her about the wondrous capacity of the human body to heal itself—an old idea that had gotten lost in the scientific shuffle along with the idea that food was your best medicine. That two-dollar consultation fee was a turnoff for most Hollywoodites— except maybe Garbo. So the little doctor from Pasadena never became rich or famous. Mecca was in Minnesota, where the Mayo Brothers did for surgery what the Wright Brothers did for flight. But there was no Institute for Noninvasive Medicine bearing Dr. Bieler's name. His legacy was an accumulation of things that didn't happen. To Gloria, among others.

Twenty years later, when a famous surgeon discovered a

tumor in Gloria's pelvis, he wanted to operate. "Thank you very much," Gloria said, getting off his examining table. She told the surgeon she intended to starve her tumor into extinction. He laughed and laughed. Then he got serious and warned her she was killing herself.

A couple of years later, she went back to see the smartass surgeon and dared him to find the tumor. When he couldn't, she said, "I hope you've learned something today. I know I have. Don't bother to send me a bill."

When it became fashionable for famous females to talk about their "lifesaving" amputations on TV, Gloria used to try to tell interviewers about the hysterectomy she didn't have. What she did to avoid it. How she starved her tumor, by cleaning herself out. She started scolding people about eating fake food and captive animal flesh. "Please, Miss Swanson," they used to say during commercial breaks, "we don't have any sponsors left. . . ."

As the star of the first hour-long talk show in the stone age of TV, Gloria was the cover girl on the very first issue of *TV Guide*. Some joke. Because what she was recommending might have been called "The *TV Guide* Diet." In other words, don't eat anything you see advertised on TV. And say no to all drugs publicized on the evening news. From aspirin to valium.

So the surgery nuts and Alka-Seltzer junkies began calling her a food nut.

Everytime a new book appeared about food and health, Gloria's bookstore would send her a copy. If she thought it was any good, she might order twenty copies for beating sick friends over the head. In 1965 she read one with the longest introduction she'd ever seen. She dashed off a postcard from Rome and sent it to the author. When she returned to New York she called him and invited him over. He was the man who came to dinner and stayed seventeen years, thereby attaining the world's endurance record in three categories: cook, lover and eventually (1976) husband.

That introduction was written by the same guy who's writing this one.

Among the oodles of ways of saying "I love you" in Japanese, one, literally translated, is: "I will cook for you." The polite response to that is usually, "I will eat your food."

So, long before Gloria and I were married, we had become a family related by blood which we created each day in our own kitchen. Today's food is tomorrow's blood.

One evening in 1971, Gloria brought young Dirk Benedict home for supper. That was the beginning of his life as a member of our family. His baptism I don't remember too vividly. There were so many of those. What I remember is his confirmation.

It was after *Battlestar Galactica* and before VCR. We were watching TV, looking at Dirk on a yacht somewhere in the Caribbean with Dinah Shore. It was very flirty-flirty. The *Enquirer* had told us that Burt Reynolds was a back number. Gloria turned her enormous blue eyes on me and demanded, "Is Dirk having a to-do-ment with her?"

I filibustered. Gloria watched talk shows like a policewoman on patrol in an all-night movie. If she noticed Joan Crawford in a sleveless gown, her upper arms flabby as hammocks, she would call her up. If she thought Tony Bennett looked smashing in his new toupee, she would call him up.

She was reaching for the phone when Dirk put on his apron for a cooking demo. While doing his stirfry, Dirk was delivering a sneaky sermonette, trashing the junk-food sponsors who would be selling their wares at the next commercial break. We were riveted to the TV screen. It was a Kamikaze attack on Madison Avenue from the offshore islands. Dirk's TVQ rating was plummeting before our eyes. "Please, Mr. Benedict," you could hear them saying, "we won't have any sponsors left."

At the finish of the show, the producers had tacked this lengthy disavowal on the crawl in big letters: "Mr.

Benedict's views are his own and do not represent those of blah blah blah. . . ."

I looked at Gloria. She looked at me. In all the years she'd been yapping and scolding, she had never earned this kind of accolade. No Oscar, no Emmy would have meant more to her. Her blazing, biting smile made it look as if she had just given birth to the boy.

On our next visit to La La Land, Dirk was locked up in the gold-plated gulag known as Universal Studios, alone on an enormous set, shooting close-ups for *Battlestar Galactica*. He couldn't get out, so Gloria corralled Ellen Graham, photographer to the stars, and we drove all the way out to the Universal lot so Gloria could give him a big hug and have it recorded for posterity.

Gloria was pushing eighty at the time. A magazine in Paris had just put her face on their cover under the screaming headlined quote, *"Je suis toujours une femme!"* "I'm still a woman." Inside, in elegant French, was the story of the hysterectomy she refused to submit to thirty years before.

Here was a happy ending, the kind she adored. At last, she said, she could happily retire—pass the torch. Now she could quit yapping about her pelvis and Dirk could start talking about his. Putting your notoriety to use, she called it. Her way of remembering Rudy.

"Adesso comincia la tortura," as Rudy used to say. "Now begins the torture." I knew Dirk would have to be tortured into writing his confessions and I knew I was going to have to administer that torture.

At first he claimed it was too soon.

For publication, maybe, I conceded. Maybe nobody's ready for a saga of spiritual development that takes place at a series of urinals. Publish it when you're eighty. Call it *I'm Still a Mensch*. But write it now. While it's happening.

"It's not good enough," he would moan on the telephone.

"You're not supposed to *read* it, idiot," I would explain. "Just let it all out. It doesn't have to be good. It only has to be true."

Then there were those eighteen-hour days with *The A-Team*. Even the stuntmen were exhausted.

"Keep a typewriter in your trailer in case you break a leg," I suggested.

"I can't write that," Dirk would plead. "It makes me look like a jerk!"

"Now we're getting somewhere," I would say. And another fig leaf would bite the dust. "We're talking terror in the toilet; give us all the grisly details."

I haunted the library in search of comforting precedents. It seemed that in English literature, nobody ever pees. Certainly not blood. Never chopped liver. And so it went.

Then my astrologer told me 1987 would be the year of the prostate. How right he was. After languishing for years on the inside pages in letters to Ann Landers and Dear Abby, the prostate was suddenly on page one. Top story on the evening news.

The surgical invasion of the President's penis with some kind of roto-rooter slicing away at his prostate gland—this "procedure," as they called it, was described to us as "routine." Even the second time around. "Normal in males of a certain age. Hundreds of thousands hold still for it every year. It's something you have to expect when you live too long."

All this comes to us from the wonderful people who brought us disinformation about Libya and Khadaffi, Iran and Khomeni, and I say to hell with it.

What we need, more than ever right now, is a minority opinion. And here it is.

William Dufty
February 2, 1987

SEVEN PRINCIPLES AND
TWELVE THEOREMS

If you suspect this book to be a total waste of your time, just another half-assed TV personality's attempt to make a quick buck . . . then tear out the following page of information and throw the rest of the Kamikaze Cowboy into the trash. *Understand* this one page, put it to practical use, and let the garbage collector peruse my excesses. For indeed, all that is written in these pages, all that has been written on any page *anywhere* is contained in these few simple principles and theorems. They have been the key to any health and happiness I've had in this lifetime.

SEVEN PRINCIPLES OF THE ORDER OF THE UNIVERSE

1. All things are differentiated apparatus of One Infinity.
2. Everything changes.
3. All antagonisms are complementary.
4. There is nothing identical.
5. What has a front, has a back.
6. The bigger the front, the bigger the back.
7. What has a beginning has an end.

TWELVE THEOREMS OF THE UNIFYING PRINCIPLE

1. One Infinity differentiates itself into yin and yang, which are the poles that come into operation when the infinite centrifugality arrives at the geometric point of bifurcation.
2. Yin and yang result continuously from the infinite centrifugality.

3. Yin is centrifugal. Yang is centripetal.
4. Yin attracts yang. Yang attracts yin.
5. Yin repels yin. Yang repels yang.
6. The force of attraction and repulsion is proportional to the difference between the yin and yang components. Yin and yang combined in varying proportions produce energy and all phenomena.
7. All phenomena are ephemeral, constantly changing their constitution of yin and yang components.
8. Nothing is solely yin or solely yang. Everything involves polarity.
9. There is nothing neuter. Either yin or yang is in excess in every occurrence.
10. Large yin attracts small yin. Large yang attracts small yang.
11. At the extremes, yin produces yang, and yang produces yin.
12. All physical forms and objects are yang at the center and yin at the surface.

If this sounds like the hopelessly mystical surrealistic jibber-jabber of one who has spent too many hours under the hot lights of Hollywood in a quasi-state of celebrity, then perhaps you are one of those who does not believe in the idea that there is such a thing as *soul* or *spirit*, who does not believe that all matter, all material things are infused with this spirit, and that spirit and matter are not two, but *one*! If so, then don't waste your limited time in this material plane we call life by reading this book. Put it down, throw it away, burn it. For indeed, you had better hurry. Time is passing. Tick, tock, tick, tock. Your metabolic clock is running down. Life will be over. You have only years, months, weeks, days, minutes, seconds, milliseconds, in which to accomplish your material goals. Hurry. Be efficient. Organized. Logical. Smart. Clever. Shrewd. Impatient. Hurry. Time is indeed tick-tocking away. For those who believe, let us continue!

PREFACE

I've had the most marvelous life. When I was sixteen my parents were divorced. At age eighteen I lost my father. By twenty-eight my career as an actor in Hollywood was finished, in the opinion of anyone who could render it otherwise. I had, at one time or another, all of the following ailments: falling hair, arthritis, acne, lower back pain, impotence, weight problems, excessive drinking habits, and finally at age thirty I achieved the American Medical Association's stamp of approval with its "discovery" of a tumor in my prostate gland.

I wouldn't have had it any other way. Remove any of these items from my physical/psychological resumé and you diminish in quantum leaps the richness of the fabric that has been my life. My joy hasn't been in spite of but because of these itemized events.

I write this while on location with *The A-Team* in Stockton, California. I am ensconced, as befits a star of my magnitude, in the local Hilton Hotel. The best Stockton has to offer. It has one feature that every hotel I stay in always has, be it $12.95/night or $200/night. That feature is a Haliburton camera case, custom-made to hold all my medicine: rice, oats, miso, seaweeds, azuki beans, sesame oil, tamari . . . all the basics. Plus a pot, a spoon, chop sticks and my trusty hotplate. All this sets up into what is always my favorite place to dine. Once again the local eateries will have to survive without any of my business.

This behavior on my part is, and has always been, considered slightly, if not grossly, abnormal. What is normal?

What numbers do we attach to normal blood pressure, normal pulse, normal cholesterol level?

Is breakfast in your hotel room without bacon and eggs abnormal? Even if it gives you that without which Grandma said you have nothing, your health?

One can have a ten-year-old tumor languishing in one's prostate and pass a physical with flying colors. I know. I did this time and again, every fall, as I had my physical for college football, and in 1969 when I took my pre-induction physical for the military. (What kept me out of the military was not a tumor in my prostate, but a severe blow to my head I'd received two years earlier playing football.) I was normal! Considering the fact that America is dropping like flies from cancer, I guess I was very much indeed a normal all-American male!

Over 24,000 American men died of prostate cancer in 1983. Over 75,000 new cases were diagnosed. It is the second most common cancer in men over sixty. American men have one of the highest prostate cancer rates in the world. Ten times greater than Japanese men. What causes it? The tumor-enlarged prostate arises in much the same way as hardening of the arteries. It is the result of overconsumption of foods rich in fat and protein such as meat, eggs and dairy. All very yang. Extremely yin foods such as sugar, refined flour products and fruits also produce fats and mucus.

Excessive eating of these extreme foods over a period of time causes an accumulation in the form of cysts or tumors. Although often benign, any enlargement of the prostate can be considered pre-cancerous, especially when discovered in someone of the ripe old age of thirty.

We as individuals are out of tune, sick. Cancer is a plague. The infinite array of modern medicines, miraculous drugs, machines, etc., are incapable of providing a cure. They can't cure cancer, diabetes, multiple sclerosis, emphysema, herpes, leukemia, AIDS. The list is endless and includes the common cold, which is, in today's medical marketplace, almost no more common than cancer (although much less profitable).

Can you find someone whose life hasn't been affected directly or indirectly by cancer? Can you find a soul on the planet earth whose life isn't affected by the threat of nuclear war?

Cancer has already become the latest "in" disease for celebrities. Scan the magazines at the check-out stand and you will find the pages loaded with countless celebrities telling of their relationship with cancer. Or how their loved one died of cancer. Or how they support the fight against cancer. Or their latest discovery of how cancer can be cured.

But the Laws of Nature have no room for favoritism. It doesn't matter what your TV-Q is, how high your weekly rating, what economic stratum you belong to, how many times you've been on Johnny Carson; when your body has had all the sinning it can handle . . . there is a wheelchair with your name on it. John Wayne, Gary Cooper, Humphrey Bogart, David Niven, Laurence Harvey, Joan Hackett, Steve McQueen, Robert Ryan, Rock Hudson—the list is endless.

People in the public eye may be of different creeds, races, sexes and professions, but they all share one not-always-so-admirable trait, an uncanny instinct for self-promotion through the latest fashion, fad, rage. And they all gather to play tennis, golf, or simply show off their wonderful talents and charm, as they raise money to "fight" cancer or any other of the growing numbers of illnesses wreaking havoc with America. Perpetuating the horrible myth that *money* can buy *health*. How many more billions will be raised before we wake up?

How soon before the celebrity ranks are so decimated that there'll be no one left to raise the millions to "fight" the battle against the enemy we so stubbornly refuse to understand is none other than our Self's own crimes against the Order of the Universe? How far off is that time when the mugger, the second-story burglar, won't be after our pocketbook or television, but rather our healthy set of kidneys, our liver, our prostate?

I recently read *The Final Chapter*, Steve McQueen's book about his battle with the Big C. If people could only read between the lines of that book, I wouldn't have the responsibility of writing this one. It's *all* there, between the lines. McQueen *didn't* make a quick exit from Cedars-Sinai Medical Center. I did. He signed the forms. And with that he "sealed his fate."

Read his adventure and you can understand what I already knew, what the process would be once I checked in. Tests upon tests upon tests upon tests. "Exploratory surgeries." Is that a vague enough phrase for you? They never tell you anything for one simple reason: *they don't know!* Or perhaps your Uncle Charlie or husband Bill or daughter Samantha has been through it and you don't need to read about it in a book.

The only thing Cedars-Sinai *knows* is that you are going to die. They are nice enough to give you your impending "check-out" date. In McQueen's case he was given two months to live.

"I can't *believe* it's over, there is so much I want to do." Those were Steve McQueen's words upon being given his very expensive "results" from Cedars-Sinai. He was right not to want to believe. It needn't have been over, nor need it be over for your Uncle Charlie or daughter Samantha.

McQueen's book is about what modern medicine can't do for you. Mine is about what an understanding of the universal laws of nature, as applied to your life via food and the principles of yin and yang, *can* do for you. Steve McQueen was one of the biggest film stars this country has ever produced. I'm just one of hundreds of television personalities made recognizable by the power of mass marketing. That isn't the only thing we *don't* have in common . . . our books have two entirely different endings. As will our lives.

No one ever doubts the procedures or diagnoses, let alone prognoses, of that contemporary institutionalized witchcraft known as the medical establishment. The American Cancer Society has us brainwashed into believing that cancer is incurable. The next step is, of course, that cancer is an *unavoidable* result of the aging process in modern-day society.

There are millions of dead and dying who are testament to the nightmare of traditional treatment of the incurable diseases that ravage contemporary America. Steve McQueen is one of hundreds who have told their story. They all have the same scenario, only the names are changed. It is time we heard from the other side of the coin.

I cannot tell you how deeply I regret that it has fallen to me to be the bearer of this unwanted good news. It astonishes no one more than myself that I should find myself in a position in which this personal story has become a necessity. Perhaps it is true that being in the public eye carries with it the responsibility of sharing your private life as payment for the material rewards and adulation they heap upon you. If so, I believe these pages fulfill that responsibility. How much more private can one get than public exposure of your biological life? Would you share your prostate with millions?

I do know that *truth* is inclusive, not exclusive, and it *is* the unavoidable consequence of those who experience it to share that experience without reservation. No matter what the personal consequences. It isn't only misery that loves company, but also *joy*. Unfortunately, there aren't many in *that* company to be kept. Being healthy and happy is a lonely road to hoe.

Dirk Benedict, actor, *The A-Team*, cancer, cure, oriental medicine, infinite freedom . . . no matter how you mix, blend and package, it's bound to be very hard to swallow. Especially for the educated arrogance of exclusive intellectuals who deduct their American Cancer Society contributions from their annual income-tax forms.

Steve McQueen was rich and famous. Because he was rich, he could afford the astronomical expense of modern treatment for his terminal disease. Because he was famous, people will buy a book about his failed attempt to survive that disease. The cost of my "cure" was less than what most people spend on diet soft drinks in one year of their guzzling lives. It is economically available to all of America. It would put modern medical megacorporations out of business.

If it weren't for *The A-Team* and my quasi-fame, this book wouldn't be published. My story from *this* side of the grave would remain as untold as those of the thousands of other poor and anonymous souls who have travelled my path before and since. If you are a member of the vast minority who are grateful that I have attempted this book, don't thank me, thank NBC and that machine in your living room that has become the galvanizing focal point of families throughout the civilized world. If this book irritates the hell out of you, don't blame me, blame the Nielsen Ratings and your inability to turn that hypnotic machine off.

Because I didn't submit to being a rat in the medical maze of exploratory surgery, everyone will question the validity of the claim that I had cancer in the first place. It must be thus. If I *did* have prostate cancer (as I most certainly did, for I have the diagnosis to prove it) and am *alive* twelve years later to preach what I practice, the ramifications are too horrifying for the general public to contemplate. The extent of this fraud and nightmarish illusion is disturbing to the very core of civilized medicine and nutrition.

Whenever the policies or beliefs or regulations of any particular area are established by a communal level of acceptability, you can know for a fact that those beliefs and policies are based on the lowest level of comprehension by the weakest member of that particular community.

That doesn't leave much room for free thinkers in the world.

Up until the past few years, anybody such as myself who held forth that the cure for sickness lies in what we eat was laughed at hysterically. And worse, was attacked as un-American, anti-Christian and just plain ol' crazy. Wacko! How stupid to think that food could be the cause and cure of our illnesses when our doctor-gurus tell us there *is no* cause for our colds, our cancers, our headaches. We wait for our "specialists" to tell us, to make up the policies and regulations by which we all live, not realizing that by the time any idea gains acceptance by an institutional body anywhere, it is almost surely passé, outmoded and far-removed from whatever the original idea was in the first place. By the time you read about something, you can be sure it is already ancient history to millions of people who *don't* listen, robot-like, to the knowing voices of their teachers, doctors, lawyers, economists, psychiatrists and dieticians.

The principles that I espouse in this little book are a testament to this fact of human nature. I write these words eleven years after the fact. All this is very old hat to me eleven years after salvaging myself from the dietary purgatory I lived in, and it bores me not a little to be quizzed as to whether I *really* believe. Or "do I still eat *that* food?" or "do I really think food can cure cancer?" It would be like asking Charles Lindbergh if he thought the airplane was here to stay or just a passing fad. Like asking Sir Edmund Hillary if he thought Mount Everest could really be climbed. Hell, he climbed the damn mountain. Do I think cancer is curable? I'm alive, ain't I?

The number of people who will believe that I wrote this

book I can count on one hand. To the hundreds of people who know me, I am not the kind of person they would cast in the role of a writer to put these words on paper.

When I came out of the carcinogenic closet some time ago and told the readers of *People* magazine that I had had prostate cancer and cured myself through the application of ancient oriental principles, it came as a magnificent shock to those people who had been close to me during the period when I was at my most cancer-ridden. Including my own family.

I didn't *behave* or *perform* like a person given the traumatic news that his prostate, at age twenty-nine, was on the terminal fritz! Many were hurt, offended, that I hadn't shared my misery with them. Or what they assumed to be a "miserable state." I wasn't miserable. I was having the adventure of my lifetime. Nothing will ever be as exciting as the journey I took with a book on yin and yang in one hand, a bag of brown rice in the other and an oversized prostate in between.

That it was to be ancient Japanese teachings of the laws of nature that were to be my saviour is merely the result of circumstance. Any of a dozen or so enlightened souls who have written down their understanding of these universal laws have all said the same thing. Only the language is different.

This book is not for those who disbelieve, who attack, who resent. There are books enough crowding the bookshelves for them. This epistle is for those who sense there *is* another way. It is time there was reading material for them. It is time there was a television celebrity reflecting their dreams. What John Wayne was to meat and whiskey is what we now need for brown rice and bancha. If you do perchance see me on TV or in the movies, observe a man well into his forties and possibly the first meat-free, sugar-free, brown-rice celebrity Hollywood has ever produced. If you like what you see, what you sense, be careful . . . you may be a prime candidate for a change in what you eat!

So often, as I sat writing this book, it struck me how easy it would have been to share my life with the reader. Chock full of biographical detail. The dates, the events, the people that chronologically document the passage of forty years. How simple and safe to share the effect, but not the cause. As is the case in almost all autobiographies.

Everyone's life is full of scrapbooks. Everyone's life is a painting with all the colors of the rainbow in it. We all have a story to tell with a beginning, a middle and eventually, an end. But the *real* story, the true through line that is our life, is not comprised of factual data detailing how we spent our time on this planet earth. The real experience is in *why* we lived our lives as we did. Not whom we married, by *why*; not where we went on vacation, but *why*; not how we achieved fame, but *why*; not whom we loved, killed, saved, cheated, but *why*.

Cause vs. effect. We are a civilization obsessed with effects. We live our lives entangled in the symptomatic chaos of never understanding the cause. Indeed, we are conditioned, taught, coerced every day of our lives not to seek answers. Health, happiness, sickness, sadness, feast, famine . . . all symptoms, effects, the cause of which we never know and are too terrified to ask.

Too terrified because the first place we must look is within. Stop all the distractions, the social whirl that comprises our daily existence, and in the silent void of aloneness, look within. Disconnect the phone; shut off the stereo, radio, TV; burn books; shun family, loved ones, friends; discharge all professional advisor, doctors, lawyers, tax accountants, nutritionists, therapists; and in the silent void that erupts, look within.

My life has been premised on a constant gaze in this direction. Macrobiotics was the compass to point me there. To end the aimless wandering. To uncover the antagonistic, complementing paradox that is our enigmatic soul.

Complementing antagonisms . . . yin and yang.

This book, then, is the macrobiological biography that hoped to share that journey.

The rest is silence.

Dirk Benedict
Bigfork, Montana
August 4, 1986

AUTHOR'S NOTE

The traditional cowboy of wild-west Americana disappeared when they slaughtered the buffalo and fenced the wide-open ranges. The fearless spirit of the Kamikaze Samurai warrior disappeared with Western influence in Japan. I don't pretend to be either a real cowboy or a real Kamikaze, but the atmosphere of my childhood in the ranching community of White Sulphur Springs in a long-ago Montana, and the self-reliant solitary discipline of my life's journey, give validity to the title of this book and perhaps new definition to both words in contemporary America. There can be a little cowboy and Kamikaze in all of us. There should be.

PROLOGUE

The great dilemma of "how to free man in spite of himself" had been the overriding concern of my father's life. With his untimely death, the great dilemma was solved and he *was* free in spite of himself. Through the happenstance of chromosomic makeup, it would fall to me, the middle of three children, to inherit the passion of his quest. What had been his through dying, I sensed with justifiable fear could only be mine through living.

There wasn't a fishing trip, a grouse-hunting expedition or a skiing trip he took me on, not even a summer's evening of playing catch with the football, that didn't involve a discussion of this great dilemma and the issues involved in it. Everyone experiences life and everyone eventually experiences death, he said. It is the manner in which they do both that is crucial. He felt that it wasn't enough just to "go through the motions" of living one's life, and he was obsessed with the discovery of the *cause* of what gave each life's motion its unique qualities.

The passion of his hunger for answers to that question made people nervous, uncomfortable . . . it made them stay away. This self-induced quarantine eventually crept into the confines of his own family. So in 1961 he found himself stranded, cut off, alone . . . except for the bespectacled presence of his sixteen-year-old middle child. During the next two (and final) years of his life, he would pour the intensely passionate culminating thoughts and ideas of his life into the captivated ears of his soul's sole audience. The heart and mind of that young audience was in turmoil as he struggled to understand the impossible . . . but there was another part of him that was religiously tucking everything away for future reference.

My father began letting go: he let go of a marriage of over twenty years; he let go of a law practice he had spent his lifetime building . . . he simply gave it carte blanche—clientele, books, typewriters, paperclips and all—to a young attorney fresh out of law school; and he let go of his pride and joy, a 1955 Jaguar sports roadster XK140 which he had spent many a winter's evening fine-tuning into a machine that would take top honors at road rallies. He let go of his home as he took to the road in a 1959 Volkswagen to finish the book he was writing in motels and hotels across the Northwest. He let go of all the material possessions that a lifetime of instinct for the finest of everything had gathered. He was ''on the road'' for the last two years of his life.

What he didn't let go of was his family. He tried, for he knew that except for the sixteen-year-old crewcut sponge at his elbow, they had let go of him. To them, as to all others who knew him, he was no longer the friend, the professional peer, the father, they had known, respected and loved. Out of my fear and inability to comprehend, I too tried to let go of this whirling dervish of philosophic oratory. I couldn't. . . .

> Life-struck, young, I crept through breathing halls
> of old museums ghosted rich with fancies sheer,
> humbly whispering, ''We seek a sanctuary here,''
> and pausing in those throbbing stalls,
> I felt the voice of BEAUTY as it calls,
> and heard it sob against the granite walls.

I couldn't let go. Was it all written and inevitable—the amount of time I would have at his side soaking up what I thought I didn't understand? Did a primal instinct for my own survival hold me prisoner, a moth to the flame of his final fiery hunger for answers? Did I know that only fourteen years later I too would begin an odyssey alone and searching for the same answers?

We fished and traveled and laughed and cried and time melted away as the torch was passed.

Sunday, August 4, 1963 . . . the sun was shining with a brightness that only the clean, clear air of Montana can allow. My father arrived at the family home to pick me up. A perfect day for fishing.

I told him I wouldn't be able to go, as I had agreed the night before to help a local rancher stack some hay.

"But we had agreed that we would spend this day together."

"I know, Dad, but it's a chance for me to make some extra money." I was going off to Whitman College in the fall and was very aware of what that would cost and that I would be the main source of providing it.

"Money? It's more important that we spend this time together."

"I just feel that since I'm going to college this fall, I should take every chance I can to earn some money."

My dad pulled his billfold out of his pocket and took three one-hundred-dollar bills out of it. Three hundred dollars that I would later learn were the sum total of his present resources.

"How much money are you going to make stacking hay?"

"Fifteen dollars."

My dad handed me the three hundred dollars. "There. Now let's go fishing."

I stood frozen on the spot. I couldn't take it.

"Son, money has no value. None whatsoever. Never put it above the living of your life. Never do anything for 'money.' If you don't stack hay today and don't make fifteen dollars, you will still go to college. And if you don't . . . if you can't afford to get a college education . . . so much the better. College isn't the answer to anything. It is only important as an experience. So instead of college, maybe you'll hitchhike through Europe or hop a steamer to some foreign country, and *that* will be the experience through which you will discover your life. But *money* has nothing to do with it. Never use it for a reason or an excuse for anything. Ever. Now, let's go fishing.''

I remained frozen on the spot. My mind tried to understand, to make a decision. I couldn't manage.

My father solved the dilemma. We never went fishing. Not that day. Never again.

It took me two years, but I finally found the words to put on the slab of marble I had placed on his grave:

George Edward Niewoehner
March 13, 1912–August 4, 1963

My father, I am yours. You keep me straight with your kind leading. Nor shall anything count for more with me than you and your good judgment, which I shall ever follow.

PART ONE

During the 1970s, Americans began to disengage from the institutions that had disillusioned them and to relearn the ability to take action on their own . . . reclaiming America's traditional sense of self-reliance after four decades of trusting in institutional help. . . .

We allowed ourselves to act as passive bystanders, handing over to the medical establishment not only the responsibilities it could handle, healing traumatic wounds and grave illnesses, but also the responsibility that in reality belonged only to ourselves, the responsibility for our health and well-being. We revered doctors as our society's high priests and denigrated our own instincts. And in response, the medical establishment sought to live up to our misplaced expectations. Placing all their trusts in the modern voodoo of drugs and surgery, they practiced their priesthood and we believed. . . .

But at various points during these last four decades, those institutions have failed us. And about ten or fifteen years ago, we began to realize this, when a string of institutional failures became blatantly apparent. At around the same time we admitted to having lost the war on poverty as well as the war in Viet Nam, we began to mistrust medicine as well. We read what were then simply incredible stories about the medical profession's routinely prescribing addictive drugs such as tranquilizers and diet pills and performing unnecessary operations . . . America's loss of faith in the medical establishment gave a strong symbolic push to the paradigm shift from institutional help to self-help. When we entered the 1970s without the long-promised cure for cancer, people began to question the omnipotence of science . . . interest in diet and nutrition soared . . . The importance of nutrition was being seriously entertained for the first time as a preventive measure against cancer . . . America's romance with running began . . . In time, we seriously considered alternatives to the medical establishment's program of annual physical exams, drugs, and surgery . . . In the 1970s we began shifting over to working on the human side, the idea being that a stronger population can better resist disease. The new emphasis on the human angle shows up in . . . the triumph of the new paradigm of wellness, preventive medicine, and wholistic health care over the old model of illness, drugs, surgery, and treating symptoms rather than the whole person.

—John Naisbitt, *Megatrends*

I know that most men—not only those considered clever, but even those who are clever and capable of understanding the most difficult scientific, mathematical, or philosophical problems—can seldom discern even the simplest and most obvious truths if it be such as obliges them to admit the falsity of conclusions they have formed, perhaps with much difficulty—conclusions of which they are proud, which they have taught to others, and on which they have built their lives.

—Leo Tolstoy (1898)

CHAPTER ONE

FLOUNDERING VAGABOND

It began, prophetically enough, in Hollywood. A city I was to come back to time and again, in sickness and in health, in success and in failure, with anticipation and with dread. But this was my first visit.

I was playing a small part in my first Broadway play, *Abelard and Heloise*, starring Diana Rigg and Keith Michel. The production was in Los Angeles for a six-week, pre-Broadway tryout at the Ahmanson Theatre.

At this point the beef, venison and elk vibrations of my first twenty-two years were still very much controlling the nature of my day-to-day activities. Arthritis was my morning wake-up call, mood swings between ecstacy and despair my daily state of mind and scotch my release from it all.

I have my routine. I'm running three or four miles a day, which everyone (this was 1971) finds quite strange. I run from the Bryson hotel on Wilshire Blvd., where the entire cast is staying, to the Ahmanson Theatre in downtown L.A. and sometimes back again after the evening performance. I have also discovered "health foods." For the first time in my mostly rural life I'm in a city with health-food restaurants! Trusting the printed word, I'm bingeing indiscriminately on anything on the menu as long as the sign out front says "HEALTH"! Hamburger, *yes* . . . but on whole wheat buns; butter, *yes* . . . but made from whole milk; eggs, *sure* . . . but direct from a roosterized chicken.

Forgetting all the time that this is just a citified version of what I had been eating while working on ranches in the big sky country of Montana, where the chickens peck in the barn

7

yard; the beef is grass-fed sans any artificial food supplementing and butchered by the rancher himself; and the milk is hand-milked from the cow and sometimes served still warm on the breakfast table. Homogenizing, pasteurizing, sterilizing are all just trick words from my sixth-grade spelling test!

But I *am* running. I *am* avoiding chemicals. I have given up refined sugar, white bread, soda pop, anything with sugar in it. This may seem mild by comparison to contemporary America's current craze for alternate "diets," but in 1971 my fellow cast members found me impossible to figure: Was I a hippie in cowboy clothing, searching like most of Southern California for a guru to pay homage to? Or was I what I appeared to be—a 190-lb., all-American, blonde-haired, blue-eyed pretender to the Redford throne? While they dabbled in far-out drugs, I played around with far-out foods. Impossible to figure.

There was one member of the cast, however, who saw in my behavior certain possibilities. One of the two stars of the show. No, not Diana Rigg (although she did flatter me and scare the horseshit off my Montana-bought Tony Lamas with an invitation to her Chateau Marmont boudoir!). Her female aggressiveness and London chic were far too much for my country shyness and Montana rustic to handle.

It was Keith Michel, who had scored a huge success in the British production of *The Six Wives of Henry VIII*, who saw nothing outlandish about my dietary dabbling. Michel was the talk of all who had known him, for he had lost thirty pounds and begun to look fifteen years younger in the two years since he had won public acclaim playing the fat and gluttonous king.

After one of the matinees he invited me for tea in his dressing room. He offered me some strange-smelling brew (bancha tea) and asked if I was interested in a bowl of rice with bechamel sauce on it. I said "no thanks." Johnny Weissmuller had a "health-food" restaurant down the block on Hollywood Blvd. and served the most wondrous vegetarian hamburgers dripping with melted cheese and all the trimmings. This, with a dish of natural ice cream for dessert, was dancing through my brain, and I was eager to get there before the evening performance. I thanked him again, but explained I had "other plans." He mentioned *macrobiotics*, yin and yang, getting rid of his migraine headaches and other maladies and said that if I was interested in really discovering health, he'd give me some books to read on the subject. I said fine. I think he sensed I wasn't ready. The literature never appeared. I never asked. Johnny Weissmuller got my business. But I'll never forget the whites of Michel's eyes. For indeed, they were *white*! None of the red veins associated with men of half his age.

The dressing room next to Michel's was occupied by Ronald Radd, a wonderful English character actor. He had overheard my conversation with Michel and took me aside the next day, poured me a double scotch, straight, and warned me to beware of Keith Michel's quack diet. I replied that he certainly looked healthy enough. "Never mind that," Radd said. He saw in this diet the ruination of true manhood. Man—by which he meant *men*—was meant to eat meat and drink whiskey, both of which Radd consumed in large quantities. "England would never have been England," he said, "if they'd all chewed the nuts and seeds and drunk the carrot juice of Keith Michel!"

I thanked him for the scotch and promised to give the matter some thought. Especially since he believed so adamantly that the lack of meat in one's diet would destroy one's ability to act! Something else destroyed his ability to act: he died of a heart attack several years later, while still in his fifties.

I think perhaps if Miss Rigg had been offering the tea and macro-snacks, she might have got what she wanted and I would have been introduced to brown rice a year earlier. But as she and Keith Michel can attest, we are only ready when we are ready.

The production opened at the Brooks Atkinson Theatre in New York in early March 1971 and got mixed, very mixed, reviews. It ran for only six weeks. During those six weeks I was living with a lovely little Jewish girl by the name of Lori whom I'd met in Los Angeles. She was from New York and had an apartment on West 72nd Street. We met while she was visiting friends in L.A., and she invited me to play house when the production returned to New York.

I was, as always, living out of a suitcase, and her offer fit right into the lack of plans I always had. I knew the old saying, "the way to a man's heart is through his stomach," but I think this girl was the first I'd ever met who sensed that the way to a man's *crotch* is through his stomach. She never complained as I dragged her time and again to some shabby, off-the-wall-and-out-of-the-way eatery, searching for the East-Coast equivalent to Johnny Weissmuller.

None of the bright, happening hangouts in and around the theatre district which are fashionable to all actors, especially employed ones, were to get any of my business. Nooks and crannies throughout Manhattan Island housed the greasy spoons for which I searched, with little Lori ever at my side. Patient and supportive in my quest for the taste I couldn't find, she never complained, as long as I ended each evening in her apartment, in her bed and in her arms.

CHAPTER TWO

NORDIC SOUL FOOD

You may not believe it, given my current professional situation, but the truth is I never dreamed of making a film or being on television. Not once. Not while stacking hay in the high mountain hayfields of Montana; not while having fun "playacting" during my college years in Walla Walla, Washington; not even while in Michigan in an English acting program for two years, taking voice, speech, movement, audition techniques and all manner of classes in preparation for a career in *acting!* Never throughout any of this did I dream and/or aspire to being in films or having any kind of celebrity status or public acclaim.

What I *did* fantasize about back in college and while in acting school was being a stage actor like Finney, Redgrave, Guinness, Olivier, Gielgud. I subscribed to the English theatre magazine *Plays and Players* and read everything I could about all the great actors, looking for the secret to their success in the craft of pretending to be other than what we are. My goal was to find a repertory theatre in this country where I could spend twenty years playing all the great parts of theatrical literature, believing that only by tackling Romeo and Hamlet could one be ready for King Lear thirty years down the road.

In May of 1971 I was astonished to find myself jetsetting my way to Stockholm, Sweden, to play the lead in a *film!* My life was becoming more film-like than any movie I had ever paid my hard-earned money to see: I had grown up in Montana without exposure to the latest films; now I was going to "star" in one. New York to Stockholm was only my third jet ride; Sweden was my first trip to a foreign country.

There were no blacks in Montana . . . this film was written by a black, produced by a black, and I was the only Caucasian in the principal cast! *Georgia, Georgia* is a film about a black night-club entertainer of international renown, currently performing in Sweden as part of her European tour. She is isolated by her fame, her race and her outspoken manner. She falls in love with a Viet Nam deserter living in Stockholm and making a living as a photographer. I played the photographer and Diana Sands the night-club singer.

Upon arriving in Stockholm, I was immediately adopted by Maya Angelou, Diana and the other blacks from America who were there ahead of me and had set up camp in one of the major hotels. It was *all* foreign to me. Blacks were new, be they from the United States or Sweden, and now for the first time in my life *whites* were new . . . Nordic whites who spoke a very strange language and behaved even more strangely. They gave new meaning to the word "withdrawn." Very different from the "howdy-partner-let-me-buy-you-a-drink-meet-my-wife-would-you-like-to-spend-the-night-where-you-from?" hospitality I grew up with. It was four weeks before I was invited into a Swedish home.

Food was a problem. For me it was a problem because Adelle Davis, my current tangent in the search for well-being, didn't translate well into Swedish, and to have "health" in Sweden was simply to chase gallons of aquavit with a sauna. Food was a further problem, because Maya was cooking!

Stooped over a stove, Maya Angelou stands over six feet! Large of frame *and* spirit. Totally outgoing, full of talk and laughter . . . strung together with poetry and song. A nonstop whirling bundle of black spirituality spreading bits of wisdom and obscenity in equal and interconnected portions. I found her irresistible. She should have played Zorba the Greek. By comparison, Anthony Quinn seemed a Catholic choirboy auditioning to be on *American Bandstand*.

Maya had written *Georgia, Georgia*. She had also written some of the music, including the title song. Her recently published *I Know Why the Caged Bird Sings* was a best seller. She was on a roll, and this little white boy from the "doo-wacka-doo" ranch country of the American Far West was in for a straight shot of rock-and-roll soul.

Diana Sands was an attractive actress in her mid-thirties with great talent. She had won an Oscar nomination for her performance in *Raisin in the Sun*. She was not happy. What for me was a smorgasbord of delights was a list of irritations to her. This was *not* her first film! Diana had been too long in the highly regimented film business of America. *Georgia, Georgia* was being shot the European way, very different from the more stratified, unionized fashion of Hollywood. This was my first film. Hell, I thought *all* films involved lots of improvisation before the director began setting up for the shots he wanted with specific camera angles. Also, the crew was small, with each person fulfilling many functions. Stig Bjorkman, the director, couldn't understand the reason for Diana's growing dissatisfaction. But Diana had a great sense of humor which, in spite of her frustration and unhappiness, would surface time and again to break the tension in its own wonderfully wicked way.

During the first few weeks, we were all thrown together: Maya cooking, Diana bitching and laughing and bitching, and the rest of the cast filling the occasional silences with their own adjustments to being black and in Sweden. And they *drank.* *We* drank. My drinking days were dwindling, and in fact, prior to Sweden I thought they were about over. But like riding a bicycle, you never forget how. So we all drank. It was the common language. The salve to ease all sores.

But *food* was a problem. Breakfast and lunch were up to us, whatever our per diem and ingenuity could manage; dinner was whatever Maya was cooking. And whatever Maya cooked . . . I ate. There was no way out. To this day I can't remember the menu. I do know this: if you were black, poor and raised in Mississippi, it was everyday fare. It was greasy and it was plentiful and it was, so I was constantly told, *soul food*!

After two weeks, I wasn't sure about my soul, but my entire digestive tract was wishing it had been born the innards of a more darkly complected young man. The irregularity and pain of my bowel movements, or lack thereof, began to have discussions with my soul. Perhaps this current fare was food for a "different" soul. A different destiny, a different lifetime. I should have known, for I had been warned. At one of our first suppers together, a member of the cast slid into the seat next to me, looked at my plate, looked at me, and said, "Right on, man, you's in the grease pot now!"

One day on the set during lunch, as I sat pondering a menu void of anything without grease, a little black man playing a small part in the film and who had been living in Scandinavia for some years, pulled up a chair next to me. "You want some *real* food?" That got my total attention. I'd had my eye on this guy for the past few weeks. His energy and good spirits were abundant and I never saw him eat. He had been a vegetarian for twenty years.

He invited me outside the restaurant and we sat on the curb while he shared his bag of nuts, raw carrot sticks, etc., and he proceeded to write down the names of three or four restaurants in Stockholm where a guy could find an alternative to the "grease pot." His name was Artie Shepherd and he had a nightclub act he performed around Scandinavia.

Artie was the second example I had met of the benefits of an awareness of what one chooses as his daily food. The absolutely perfect timing of his appearance in my life—to encourage me, point the way and save me from the despair of endless floundering as I searched for answers—was the first of many such "coincidences" that led to the fulfillment of my personal dream.

With Artie I began to know that there are no such things as coincidences. Accidents are never accidents, but always have cause, reason and are exactly what we deserve. What we call good luck and bad luck we do so merely out of ignorance of the reality of our particular situation in life.

Once we initiate direct action toward the realization of a dream and totally commit our mind, soul and body, then the most miraculous and unforeseeable forces come into play and aid us in the realization of that dream.

Meeting Artie Shepherd would be the first of countless "coincidences" that would propel me beyond what I dreamed myself capable of being and achieving.

CHAPTER THREE

MY MISS SWEDEN

It was several days after meeting Artie Shepherd that I decided it was time to make my escape from the grease pot. I got my own apartment and began cooking my own breakfast, tapdancing for lunch and romancing for dinner.

Monica Maltentoft was her name. She may not have won Miss Sweden, but I failed, and not for want of perusing, to find an imperfection. True to her ancestry, co-mingled with the burden of being beautiful, she was very hard to get. Forget icewater in the veins, this girl had icebergs bobbing. And of course all this disdain only fanned the flames of my desire for her. I oozed as much charm as every fiber of my being could muster. I tried everything, including humility. Nothing. And just as I gave up all hope, the iceberg melted. And what a melting there was! For reasons she kept stoically to herself, Monica chose me as the person on which to unleash the long-smoldering fires deep in her Icelandic hearth. Many months later I was to pay a price for her passion in spiritual and emotional pain, but the immediate consequences were physical.

Shortly after she had chosen me as the paramour of her life, we were having dinner in a fashionable Stockholm bistro. There was music, candlelight, wine. What the hell, I thought, why not a big, juicy, macho steak?

Hours later, as Monica rolled back the sheets and waited, I stared at the bottom of a Swedish toilet bowl (which didn't look the least bit foreign) and vowed never again to eat anything from the Kingdom of Animal! It was an evening without romance.

Breakfast the next morning was my usual: brown rice with

an egg cracked over it for the last three minutes of cooking. I felt better. So did Monica.

Filming continued. So did the brown rice and the romance. Diana drank more and her mood swings became increasingly severe and erratic. I remember thinking, and it was the first time I had made such a connection, that perhaps she was not well! Not well physically . . . hence her strange behavior. About two years later she died of cancer. A romance with which I was yet to have.

It was in Sweden, shortly after I quit eating animal flesh, that I began to notice the changes: first and foremost, the arthritic pain in my knees, which I had had since age sixteen, went away. Disappeared! Did *not* subside and/or diminish; no, *vanished*! That was, as anyone who has suffered from this nagging disease can attest, a bonafide miracle. It took about ten days. I awoke one morning with the most tremendous sense of well-being and energy. Literally bounced out of bed and felt so good I wanted to explode. The sensation was so strong that it was eerie. Was this a dream? And then it hit me . . . no *pain*! No deep bending of the knees to get them to begin to release the throbbing ache that was always there. I was astonished. My hands, too, were free of the usual stiffness. Well, I was a believer.

What I didn't realize, had no inkling of, was the frightening energies frozen in my body that I was on the verge of melting. Thre was no method to my madness . . . no understanding of the forces at work. I had only a vague sense of direction, away from animal food and toward anything else. I began to lose weight. When I look at the film *Georgia, Georgia*, I can see, as anyone can who looks, which scenes were shot first and which came later in the shooting schedule. Cheekbones began to appear. My jawline defined and the predictions of stardom commenced.

I knew physical things were going on, changing. What I didn't was how dangerous all this was . . . what a bomb was waiting to go off. For twenty-six years I had been eating animal food three times a day, and for twenty-two of those twenty-six years much of that animal meat had been "wild," in the form of venison and elk. Now all of a sudden I quit, completely, "cold tofu"! *Not giving* my system what it had been used to for all those formative years. Well, it didn't take long. Six weeks later, in a villa on the Greek Island of Leros, the bomb exploded.

But I'm getting ahead of myself . . . we're still in Sweden and every day is like being *reborn*. It's interesting to me that I use that phrase so many times when referring to my entire twelve-year journey with food as medicine . . . "It was like being reborn." How many times can one be "reborn"? The fact is that over and over again it did feel like a new awareness, another starting over. Like peeling an onion, there is always another layer. Just when you think you have finally found your true skin, lo and behold, another layer appears, another fog lifts from your eyes. I have come to realize that the process, the journey, *is* endless, and that is how you know you are in harmony with the universe, the Divine. We end each day by dying and are reborn as we rise the next morning from being dead asleep. Each day is a lifetime, and the ultimate rebirth is experienced in the form of what we call *death. Death*, the ultimate *beginning*.

Each day of that summer in Sweden was an ecstasy. The pain in my joints was gone . . . and there were other changes. The love of my Swedish sojourn was to reap the rewards of one of them.

My sex drive had always been strong. Why shouldn't it be? I was young, strong and had grown up where there was a scarcity of women . . . a wonderful combination to create very strong male/female attraction. So when it came to sex, there was another "rebirth" for me in the arms of Monica, my Swedish volcano.

There is something to that, you know: the fact that rural Montana's paucity of women created a strong craving for their company. Lack of supply creates demand. Ask any guy who's been on the Alaskan Pipeline, or in any trench in any war . . . women take on an unbelievable significance. If I had my way, boys and girls would be raised separately and fed different foods until they were sixteen years old. This would create a strong attraction and appreciation for members of the opposite sex. Have you ever met a girl who was fresh out of an all-girl college? I have! I rest my case.

So I have always loved and been drawn to women with a zeal born out of years in the company of men, doing what men do: work and talk about their female fantasies. Sweden was a fantasy come true and Monica was its ultimate personification. We leapt into each other's arms in a desperate attempt to fulfill each other's sexual fever pitch. I had a lot to learn.

Forgetting the first few years of post-adolescent floundering with buttons and straps and nono's that mean yesyes in anxiety-ridden sessions downstairs, trying not to wake the parents, or in the back seats of '53 Chevys; forgetting all that playing at foreplay . . . I can't say I ever suffered from premature ejaculation, although there are several girls who would swear I did or might as well have. It isn't a matter of age, either, although prior to the summer of 1971 I would have agreed with those who maintain that "control" comes solely with experience.

On one level, sex is a purely physical feat, like running a race or throwing the discus. Your time or distance doesn't improve with age. In truth, with age one usually gets slower and weaker, not vice versa. And anyway, what I experienced all happened at the age of twenty-six. The only variable was what I was *eating*.

In the summer of 1971 I went from the sexual hundred-yard dash to the mile. (The marathon was some years down the road.) I remember distinctly the first time the love-making continued. There was a stack of records on the turn-table ("If music be the food of love"), and at the passionate moment of vaginal entrance, Ravel's *Bolero* began. The next thing I remember is descending from the clouds to the last strains of Mr. Ravel's masterpiece and the dying whimpers of my beloved Monica. Two masterpieces ending in perfect unison. Monica was astonished. And grateful! I was astonished and, as is my nature, curious! I somehow sensed, though I took any credit she felt like giving me, that I had nothing to do with this feat of endurance.

At the first opportunity, for later documentation, I timed Ravel's *Bolero* in order to have a precise record of this Olympian effort. Twenty-three minutes! It *was* a record. For me, at least, and over double my previous best. With the national average for the American male at two to three minutes from beginning to end, I felt sure this belonged in the *Guinness Book of World Records*!

Maintaining an erection is a matter of endurance. I wonder now why it took so many years for that idea to come to me. It seems perfectly obvious that in the sexual act, like any physical endeavor, the longer you can sustain an increase in your pulse and blood pressure while maintaining an optimum oxygen uptake level, the longer you can continue. Endurance. Aerobics. There are foods that build strength and foods that encourage endurance. That summer, as I stopped eating animal flesh and increased my intake of complex carbohydrates, my ability to ''endure'' any and all physical enterprises increased. This was all very bewildering to me, as I had no understanding of the reasons why. I was merely aware of the changes, the only significant variable being what I was eating. The fact that I had always been very active was of tremendous benefit. I grew up on hard labor, played high school sports and college football and began running (before the term ''jogging'' was invented) in 1967.

So I was very tuned in to my body's ability to perform in any physical arena. Including the sexual one. I'd always found it a great source of frustration that I couldn't control in any meaningful way the time it took to reach a climax. I assumed that somewhere up above, God held a stopwatch and simply said, at His whim, "That's it, you've had enough fun. *Wham*, it's over." I can only remember always wanting it to last longer. Imagine what my partner was wanting? It never entered my head that one could better one's time in the sack just as surely as one could better one's time on the track. Much less, that diet could have anything to do with it.

But there I was, in my twenty-sixth summer, camped in Stockholm, of all the perfect places, adding minutes by the score to my sex life and miles to my daily run through the beautiful countryside. And all I'd done was say "no" to food of animal origin and "yes" to any alternative I could find . . . which turned out to be complex carbohydrates.

The body runs on carbohydrates. Not protein. It also funs on carbohydrates. If sex were a matter of sheer strength, increasing one's intake of meat would be beneficial. It isn't, it's a matter of maintaining a high level of physical exertion over an extended period of time.

My pulse when I was playing college football was in the mid-seventies. My blood pressure was 130/80. Today my standing pulse is around 45 and has been as low as 39 when free of coffee, alcohol and the sedentary lifestyle of working on a television series. My blood pressure is 106/60. So, after jumping rope for fifteen minutes, or running for thirty minutes, or making love for an hour, my pulse and blood pressure have a long way to go before exhaustion sets in. The body is just cruising. As the quality of the blood changes, so does its ability to carry and exchange oxygen as it flows through the body, fueling the most remote regions on its journey.

Monica was in love with me and my new-found stamina. I was in love. I was in ecstasy. With no pain in my joints, I had plenty of room for the pain of romance. Life had never been better. Sweden, glorious summer, in love, money in my pocket, health like I'd never had in my entire life . . . it's no wonder that the making of the film *Georgia, Georgia* became almost a hobby.

It was here that I realized any acting I was to do in this lifetime would have to fit into wherever my life was leading me. My fantasy of one day taking over where Olivier and Gielgud left off began its long slide into the vague memory it is today.

There was something I didn't realize then. I wasn't to learn it until later. It was that every upside has a downside, and vice versa; yin must be followed by yang as night follows day. Every front has its back, and the bigger the front, the bigger the back.

I didn't know that in Stockholm in 1971. I know it now, a dozen years later, sitting in my celebrity status motor home on location with *The A-Team*. Yes sir, the bigger the front, the bigger the back. The realization of that has released me from a thousand anxieties during the last twelve years. And now, as I sit pecking away on my machine, waiting to be called to woo some Hollywood starlet in front of a whirring camera, preserving on film some writer's fantasy of what it would be like to always get the girl, I know that all this success—all the acclaim of being in a successful television show, making more money in one year than my lawyer father made in his lifetime, being told I *am* as suave, charming and perfect as that writer's fantasy—all this avalanche of all-American-on-top-of-the-heap *success* holds within itself the fertile seed which will germinate its opposite. Just as each day has its darkest moment and its brightest; each season its deepest winter day and gentlest summer afternoon; each relationship its agony and its ecstasy; just as surely will all this full-blown material success and notoriety give birth at some future point in time to unemployment and rejection, both professionally and publicly. There will be a new show, a new kid on the block. I will, *The A-Team* will, be yesterday's news. Within each youth lies the inevitable old person they will become. *The bigger the front, the bigger the back.* The higher our weekly ratings, the farther it is to the bottom of the list. The more public acclaim we hunger for and struggle to achieve, the more profound personal aloneness we bring upon ourselves. There is no escaping it. He who insists on being first will be last, and "the meek shall inherit the earth."

Life in the fast lane quite often denotes a personal, spiritual standing still. In youth, we think everything lasts forever; and when it doesn't, we despair. In that despair a million acts of desperation manifest themselves. They run the gamut from the international wars struggling to maintain national supremacy, number one in the world, to having the face lifted, struggling to maintain the "appearance" of youth well into middle age. Let it go. Let it be. Let it change. For no matter how many world wars are fought, no matter how many tucks are taken . . . there *will* be *change*. The bigger the front, the bigger the back.

With the acknowledgement of this universal law comes *humility*. That is to say, it becomes part of us. Not as a quality of our personality that others can comment on and applaud us for, but a *humility* which is in our bones as much as blood is in our veins. We don't "act" humble, we *are* humble. Consequently it emerges from us without our realizing it. We understand the temporal quality of each moment in our life and that it will absolutely move into the next moment as we pass through and on and into the next lifetime. And the worldly quality of each of these moments, be it fame and fortune or anonymity and famine, will pass.

I hadn't yet learned humility in Sweden. I still thought there could be gain with no pain, enlightenment without disillusionment, and that I could go from my years of meat-eating to grains without any atonement for what had gone before.

But only a few weeks later, on the Greek island of Leros, I was to learn differently.

CHAPTER FOUR

DRIVING TOWARD DESTINY

The cinematographer on *Georgia, Georgia* was a wonderful Greek fellow: Andreas Bellis. Living in exile, like many of Greece's artists during the military regime of Papadopoulos, Sweden was the refuge for him and his beautiful Greek girlfriend, Despina. She was a well-known actress in Greek films and had been forced to flee the country. Andreas had been doing well in Scandinavia's film industry due to his wonderful talent and even more wonderful personality. He was a man who exuded a love of life and the capacity for the spontaneous enjoyment of each day. Andreas loved to laugh. He had suffered great misfortune due to his country's recent upheaval, but like those with a large spirit and a zest for life, you would think he hadn't a care in the world.

Upon completion of filming, July 15, 1971, Andreas planned to return to Greece and gain custody of Despina's son. The two of them were determined to get her son out of Greece so that he could live with them in Sweden. Their journey, Andreas warned me, would not be without certain perilous possibilities. He needed to say no more, I was hooked! I had to go along.

Looking back I realize he was glad to have me come along, not only because of our new friendship and the fact that we genuinely enjoyed each other's company, but also because it wouldn't hurt to have an American along to provide a smokescreen. The trip was to be made by car . . . a brand new Jaguar sedan. I questioned Andreas on the wisdom of driving so conspicuously into a country that had his name on its list of "undesirables!" Wasn't a more low-profile mode of transportation better suited to his plan, which included abducting his girlfriend's son? It was precisely the astonishing bravura of driving into his former country in full view and in such an attention-getting car that would guarantee success, he argued. They'd never expect such a thing. And I was just the right touch, a rich American kid on vacation with friends. This would allow us to pass through countless check stations without in-depth scrutiny.

Andreas was right. We drove the length of Sweden to the port city of Malmo, where we crossed the channel into Germany. Then down through the middle of Europe into Northern Italy, continuing south to the port of Brindisi, where we caught a ferry to Patreus, Greece, with a layover in Corfu. At every border we were checked, and each time the combination of a dazzling Jaguar, the young American at the wheel, beautiful Despina, hidden mysteriously behind Gucci sunglasses, and Andreas with a Borsalino, sitting enigmatically alone in the back seat, did the trick. I did most of the talking, even though it required an interpreter for languages both Andreas and Despina spoke fluently.

It wasn't until Brindisi that we ran into problems. The Italian honcho at the office where you get tickets for the ferry over to Greece was no dummy. He knew exactly what he had sitting in front of him. Two Greeks desperate to get back into their homeland. Round trip. They were coming to get something, to see somebody. He also assumed, due to the flashy sports car and our nouveau riche attitudes, that we had *money*. Despina with her Greek imitation of Jackie Onassis; me with my blonde-haired, blue-eyed American sheen; Andreas with his blasé demeanor and film-director attire . . . it all backfired. The Italian knew we were loaded. He smiled his oily smile and was so sorry, but there were no more spaces available. We asked if he was absolutely sure? He'd see what he could do. Could we check back with him later in the afternoon? Certainly. We did. He had "managed" to find one last space, but it would be expensive. He was right. Seems he'd had to bribe so-and-so, who had to bribe so-and-so, etc., and it was all passed along to us . . . where the buck finally stopped. A fee that was easily quadruple the normal price. But at least we had our ticket for a space on the boat.

It was late afternoon. Boarding wasn't until 7:00 P.M. We went to a little café for espresso and conversation until the appointed hour. When we finally arrived and pulled into the line of automobiles getting ready to board, it appeared to me that there were way too many for the size of the boat. As we inched closer to the head of the line, it seemed more and more apparent that my instincts were right. When we reached the front, we could see that there were only two parking spaces left on the ship.

The Italian official at the point of boarding was a sight to behold and one I will never forget. He was *soooo* handsome! Tall, lean, dark hair, blue eyes and dressed in an impeccable white uniform with gold braid. He looked at our passports, etc., and smiled. Seems there was a problem. Why were we going to Greece? Where had we come from? Were Despina and Andreas residents of Greece? Why Swedish passports? Did the name Stassinopoulas mean anything to them? The questioning went on. The minutes ticked away. I was sweating. I could see Andreas was struggling to remain calm. Despina refused to speak, to even look at the official. The Italian told us to wait a bit. He went to the car behind us, spoke with them briefly and then waved them onto the ferry. They drove around us, onto the loading ramp and down off the pier into the ship's hold. One space was left.

While the guard was at the other car, Andreas told me to get behind the wheel and to drive onto the boat when he waved to me. He then got out of the car and began to speak with the guard, in Italian and very fast. The official abruptly walked away and motioned the next car behind us to pull around us and board the ship. Andreas waved. He then stepped in front of the other car, which had to stop, and I pulled past and onto the ship. As I drove down into the hold, Andreas jumped onto the boarding ramp and followed us. There was a lot of screaming and shouting from behind us. The boarding ramp began to rise. We were on the ship. The hatch was being closed and I could still hear the impossibly handsome official yelling. Andreas assured Despina and myself that nothing would happen now, that the Italians would not bother going through the delay and effort involved in trying to get us back off the ship. Especially since there was, in fact, nothing illegal about our papers, other than the price we'd had to pay. He was right. We found ourselves Corfu bound, enroute to Athens.

I remained in Greece and/or the Greek Isles until mid-September, and every trip, every meeting at a restaurant, every visit to any social gathering—even dinners in the private homes of newfound friends—were all carried out in this cloak-and-dagger atmosphere, some of it imaginary, some of it real. More real than I could have imagined.

I found myself living on the island of Leros, a small piece of land just north of Rhodes, from which one can see mainland Turkey. My dear friend Stig Bjorkman had a second home there with his girlfriend, Sun Axelson, a well-known Swedish novelist. They were the only other "foreigners" on the island, except for an English sculptor, Michael Piper. I say "foreigners," but in truth they all spoke fluent Greek and had lived in Greece (off and on) for fifteen years. Michael, who was in his fifties, had spent most of his life on the Greek Islands, moving farther and farther east, away from the growing onslaught of tourism, beginning in the early fifties on Mykonos and ending in 1971 in Leros.

A note on Leros: in those days you couldn't find it mentioned in any Greek Chamber of Commerce Guides to the islands. They didn't want foreigners visiting. Historically, going back thousands of years, the island was said to be inhabited by evil spirits. All mental patients are shipped to this island. During the military takeover, a large concentration camp was constructed there to house thousands of political prisoners. In 1971 there were still twenty or so prisoners who were considered dangerous to the current regime. It was no one's garden spot.

But to me and my Greek/Swedish friends it was a garden of Eden. And to the native Greeks, many of whom had lived there for generations, it was the *only* island in the Aegean. Personally, I never wanted to leave. I rented a house, actually a villa, for twelve dollars a month, just down the hill about a hundred yards from Stig and Sun's beautiful house. It had been built by wealthy Egyptians in 1939 as a vacation home. The war took care of their vacation plans, and the house had passed from one owner to another over the years. It was huge, with a walled-in courtyard, fifteen rooms and a view from the veranda that included Turkey. It was somewhat in need of repair, but that only appealed to my Montana "fixer-up" nature.

Sound like paradise? It was. But every front has its back, as I was just about to learn. Here on Leros, in paradise, I was about to find hell.

CHAPTER FIVE

BORN IN MONTANA, BREAD IN GREECE

In retrospect, one of the main reasons I loved Leros so much was that it offered an environment free from the endless variety of junk foods one is accustomed to being constantly tantalized with elsewhere. How difficult it is to find a place in today's world where The Big Mac and Kentucky Colonel haven't set up house! Food was very simple on the island.

Leros had a local bakery you could smell a mile before you could see. The grain was ground by stones a hundred years old. Inside it was like a huge granary, with piles of grain in one corner, stacks of fresh bread in another and the stones in the middle. The ovens were also made of stone and at one time had been fueled with wood. So with one gaze you could see the entire process, from the whole grain to the finished loaf. The place became a daily ritual in my island meanderings, and soon I couldn't get through a day without an aromatic fix.

Bread had always been a source of concern to me. It was mentioned in every book I had ever read. From the Bible to Hemingway to Philip Roth to Neil Simon to Jackie Susann. The one food *everyone* ate. I've never met anyone who didn't like bread. My college peers even used the word as slang for money. I, personally, could never ever get enough of it. No matter what my main course—veal, venison, trout, pheasant, T-bone—I always mixed it up with, chased it down with, slice after slice of bread.

Very early I was made aware that, as in all things, there is a difference in quality when it comes to bread. My father bought a simple, hand-cranked flour mill. He then went to the local farmer and bought whole wheat in a fifty-pound sack, and this was in the mid-fifties, when the entire country was turning to the "miracle" of vitamin-enriched, scientifically improved "wonder" bread. Bread which gave new meaning to the word "white" and/or "refined." My father's insistence on having his bread freshly ground, freshly baked and devoid of any man-made "improvements" only added to his growing reputation as a heretic. When I was seven or eight, I can remember him speaking of the divine wisdom that went into the creation of grain in its natural state and saying that the act of milling the grain into flour was brutal enough, refinement enough, to assuage our insatiable desire for complicating simplicity, and that the less mankind improved it, the better off we would be.

You can perhaps imagine—though I doubt it—how such un-American proselytizing inflamed the local populace during this safe, sane Eisenhower/McCarthy era. Although my father is long gone, his 1955 hand-cranked flour mill is in my log-cabin pantry today, still doing what he dreamed it would. That's a kind of immortality, and certainly the continuation of a dream. Had my old man been J. Paul Getty, he couldn't have left me a richer legacy.

More than the arts—television, film, theatre, etc.—*bread* I believe reflects the condition of a society. Consider the process by which a typical commercial bread is made in America: a complete grain, with mineral, protein, carbohydrates and an outer husk of roughage, is subjected to a long and expensive refining process during which the mineral, protein, carbohydrates and bran are *separated* from one another and/or destroyed, leaving only white flour, with which various products (from bread to Twinkies to croissants to Aunt Jemima Pancakes) are made. *Then* we "enrich" the bread by scientifically adding (in theory) all the vitamins and minerals necessary for good health. No wonder they call it Wonder Bread!

Even if one accepts the idea that man can recreate a whole

food better than nature did, even if it were true that all this processing helped the final product, it is still madness. Taking wholeness, tearing it asunder, putting it back together and calling it "new and improved" is psychotic! Is it any wonder that mental disease is rampant and afflicting human beings at ever-younger ages, or that *finally* traditional medicine is beginning to recognize the link between hyperactive children, schizophrenia, etc., and vitamin deficiencies? That they then prescribe vitamin supplements is, of course, more insanity, but at least it's a recognition of the cause. And if one suggests ingesting whole, untampered food, one is considered a "nut"!

The *real* nuts are those Madison Avenue gurus who help General Mills and Kellogg hoodwink the public into thinking they're making food for health instead of the real reason . . . to make masses of *money*. Because General Mills knows best—knows best how to make almighty billions out of what should be, what could be, *free* to us all . . . *food*! Look at any of the hundreds of packages of breakfast cereal in any supermarket in any city in this country. If you can't see the cruel joke involved in this, then you get what you deserve when you pour that stuff into your family's bellies and wonder simultaneously why Johnny can't read, Sally has split ends at age twelve, and hubby has migraines. All those fantastic colored boxes that sell you free trips to Hawaii or promise free prizes inside are hiding the sick *fact* that there is very little food inside. You would be better off to eat the box itself. Just read the ingredients—if you can get past the mumbo jumbo they use, the seven-syllable chemicals involved and the word games to make you *think* there isn't any sugar included (except *brown* sugar)—and see if you can find anything you've ever seen growing in Grandma's garden! As its bread goes, so goes the nation.

It's all exterior, facade, glamour, show . . . very little substance, truth. We've reached a point where people no longer *know* what an honest-to-God carrot tastes and looks like. They don't grow nice and straight like the ones you get in the supermarket. Nothing in the universe grows nice and straight. Life is an adventure for a carrot, just as it is for you and me. It ain't easy to grow! Sometimes there's too little moisture and sometimes too much, and sometimes sandy soil and sometimes too little sun, and that *shapes* you, gives you character, bends you. But you survive and are stronger and wiser for it. You have evolved. And a people fed on hot-house vegetables, feed-lot beef, fish-farm trout, etc., all grow in an environment insulated from the natural cycles of nature, become hot-house people. Weak, degenerating to the point where we have kids in the strongest years of their lives who must live in bacteria-free bubbles because they have no "natural" defenses against *life*! Against the natural elements of life.

Buy a bag of whole wheat or oats or barley or rice or corn or rye or buckwheat and you can bypass all of Madison Avenue. With one inexpensive purchase you can cut out all the middlemen making fortunes off your bankrupt health and the health of your offspring, not to mention the destruction of the future of this planet, which depends on the *wholeness* of the human beings populating it.

The Pepsi Generation will go down in infamy, even more infamous than the Wonder Bread generation of my parents. But beware. Madison Ave., corporate America, Big Brother, are watching, and as they see more of you question, more of you wanting control over what you eat, your own health, your own lives, they jump on that bandwagon, too. They keep right on tearing apart the lonely grain of wheat, but sell it back to you in all its separate parts: wheat germ . . . wheat bran . . . lecithin . . . whole-wheat flour . . . white flour. Fragmented food . . . fragmented mentalities . . . fragmented earth.

The brain is a mechanism fed with oxygen and blood.

Contaminate the blood and you contaminate every area to which it flows, especially something as infinitely delicate as the human brain. If Sigmund Freud had given up his sugar (and heroin) addiction, he would have, perhaps, glimpsed the futility of his life's work. It's no small wonder he refused to partake of that which he prescribed for all mankind: psychoanalysis. Was he above it, afraid of it, or did he know it would never cure anyone of any mental disease?

Any sober alcoholic knows that his drinking days were days lived in a fog, and sobriety was like being reborn. Ditto for those millions of kids sitting down to their sugared pops and fruit circles and frosted loops every morning before school. From kindergarten on, they learn in a chemically induced fog. The contamination, the degeneration—physical, mental, psychological—begins in the blood stream. As its bread goes, so goes the nation. The contamination of a nation begins in its blood stream. Contami-*nation*!

I don't think one ever forgets the truth. It reverberates forever, and the extent to which one doesn't follow those vibrating echoes is the same degree to which sickness and disease spread throughout one's physical, emotional and spiritual life. Once we know better, we must do better. And so that little organic bakery in the far-off land of Leros, Greece, brought back the words of my father along some trout stream in the mountains of Montana, twenty years earlier, speaking of the eternal truth in whole-grain bread.

I don't let General Mills interfere between what God created and what I put into my body. No Sugar Pops for me. I'm off that hook and the hook of all the physical and psychological crutches we're conditioned to believe we *need* to have a happy life. So my father's hand-cranked flour mill remains very active in my life, and although I don't eat much bread these days (I'd rather eat the grain whole; even milling is a refinement my soul no longer craves), it reminds me of the origin of original sin.

CHAPTER SIX

LETTING GO

August on the island of Leros. A Garden of Eden surrounded by the silky blue Mediterranean Sea. Eating simple foods. Spending my days walking or cycling around the island, swimming in the endlessly caressing waters that held such a powerful grasp on my imagination. It was very strong medicine to a boy from the high and dry mountains of far-away Montana who had never been closer to this kind of romance than old issues of the *National Geographic*!

My Swedish bombshell had had to remain in Stockholm to fulfill modeling commitments. Not having her 36-24-36 inches of seductive passion with me in this paradise proved to be a blessing in disguise. My Garden of Eden had no Eve. Had Adam been so lucky he would not have tasted the sweet treat that began all the dualistic nonsensical thinking that begat the idea of good vs. evil and an endless stream of guilt-breeding religious institutions ever since.

Leros was certainly to be my Garden of Eden, for it was here, as I have said, that the first huge step back to *zero*, back to the point of original sin, was to be taken.

As I walked, cycled and ran the terrain of Leros and swam in its waters, I felt an ever-growing sensation of expectancy. As if I were waiting for something, some event, and all my daily activities were preparations for that happening. It was not long in coming.

In mid-August, after nearly two weeks on the island, the serene status quo was mildly changed by the appearance of two tourists. Two American youths of college age who were knapsacking through the islands, trying to avoid the more usual tourist haunts. It was therefore inevitable that they would find Leros, one of the most untouched islands in the Greek chain. Naturally, they were quick to meet the only other English-speaking people on the little island and were invited to spend a couple of days by Stig and Sun.

They were "health nuts." In their knapsacks were a minimum of clothes and a maximum of various food items, prominent among which were several pounds of brown rice. They ate two dinners at the house and for each cooked a main dish that had the brown rice as its main ingredient. It was true then and it's true today, fifteen years later: I couldn't get enough of the stuff. It is a craving that goes back centuries, I think, and is the very essence, soul, of hunger for a fuel that will propel me farthest along my evolutionary path. Meat ties you to the earth; grain ties you to the stars, the universe.

In short, I overate at both meals. The second was to be my undoing, or more correctly, the beginning of my *doing*. About the food itself, I remember only a large wooden bowl in the center of the table to which I kept going back for more. As was usually the case, we had eaten late, not beginning until around eight-thirty in the evening. I had no ill sensations after dinner, in spite of the fact that I must have consumed at least four plates *full* of rice. Satiated, yes . . . but not nauseous, as is usually the case with gluttony.

All meals with my European friends were followed by hours of conversation, a practice I truly loved and find missing in most fast-food, on-the-run, American get-togethers. Always racing to catch an opening curtain, a film, a business appointment, get to bed early so as not to miss the 6:30 A.M. exercise class, get the car before the parking lot closes, get off the streets before the muggers come out and on and on and on. But in Leros, food and the eating of it *was* the entertainment of the evening, and discussion of any and all subjects followed. The night I ate myself into oblivion was no exception. Around twelve-thirty I said my good-nights, thanked our American guests for their company, apologized for hogging all the rice and returned to my Egyptian villa, one hundred or so yards down the hill nearer the beach.

I fell asleep immediately, which must have been around 1:00 A.M. I awoke about thirty minutes later as if coming out of a very deep, deep, profound sleep full of voices, none of which I could remember once awake. It was a gradual awakening, and some minutes before I became aware of what had been the reason for the interruption of my nocturnal rest. I must say that I have always been a very coordinated, graceful sleeper. By that I mean I can go to sleep under any conditions. Nothing bothers me once it is time to rest. Not lights, not noise, not an aroused female, a barking dog, thunder and lightning . . . when I sleep, I sleep. I've slept standing up, sitting down, on buses, and even, on several occasions, while driving my car. Once in 1979 I slept through the worst rainstorm in a couple of decades in California and woke up, stepped out of my bed and into a foot of water. The entire apartment had flooded through a door that had blown open in the middle of the night. So for me to be awakened for no immediately apparent reason was unusual.

It took several minutes before I gradually sensed the reason for my sleep being disturbed. I felt nauseous. Very slightly, but definitely nauseous. Like the sound a train makes when you first hear it in the distance. But unlike the train, I had no sense of direction, no sense that the queasiness was either getting worse or fading. I got up, thinking that I had just overeaten and my stomach was letting me know it didn't appreciate my lack of discipline. I drank a glass of water from the bottle in the next room and returned to bed and in about five minutes or so was once again asleep. No harm, no foul. Or so I thought . . . the truth was to be quite the contrary.

As is always the case with those events we wonder how

we lived through, I am glad I had no inkling of what was to come, nor do I pretend now that an amateur writer such as myself can begin to express it with the written word. But at any rate . . . thirty minutes later I again awoke. I felt sick much more rapidly this time. The train was definitely coming toward me. *Merde!* I thought. I *am* sick. The flu? Food poisoning? Gluttony? Well, I've been sick before, it's unpleasant, but I'll live through it. I gritted my already gnashing teeth, sipped some more water and once again laid my body down.

I drifted once again into sleep. It didn't last long. I awoke. Abruptly this time, with the immediate recognition of the fact that I was indeed not well. The train was not only approaching at a horrendous rate, but seemed, in fact, about to run right over me. I saw no way of getting off the tracks.

A doctor? I wasn't sure there was one on the island, and my Montana Kamikaze Cowboy upbringing still echoed with the slogan that we must handle our bad times ourselves. Neighbors were often thirty miles away if you had trouble in the mountains while hunting or broke a leg while irrigating the hay fields. My neighbors in this case were a hundred yards away. It might as well have been thirty miles.

On this third awakening, I felt immediately vomitous. I rose from my bed, which took enormous effort, and headed for the front door of the villa. I felt as if the entire weight of the house was on my back. I ached. I also knew, as any violently seasick landlubber does, that upheaval was near. I was right. I reached the courtyard just in time to relieve myself.

You know how sometimes when you're sick, you want to throw up but can't quite and only hope you can, because you know you'll feel better? So you resort to fingers down the throat to assist the process. Well, this was nothing like that. It came out of me pronto. In volumes. For minutes it lasted, until I knew that only my intestines themselves remained to be regurgitated. I had nothing to say in the matter. It was a puke to end all pukes. It felt as if the first morsel of food I ate as a child had finally been heaved up, along with everything else in between.

As the heaving stopped, it took several moments for the world to come back into focus. I began to grasp at the idea that now I would feel better. The worst was over. Whatever it was that had caused this had been evacuated. I would listen to the train fade into the distance as well-being seeped back into my now emptied, drained body.

Little did I know how much more was to come!

My first awareness, as I surfaced and the world did finally gain focus, was of being weak. I had never, not even during my worst adolescent indulgence in Apple Andy wine, been so wracked by the physical act of regurgitation. I felt so weak. I must lie down again, I thought, and attempted to climb the veranda steps into the house. Halfway up the steps, the feeling of nausea again began to stir in my guts. My God, I thought, this can't be. Not after that, not so soon. What is going on here? Redemption is never easy. But what had I done to deserve this?

I sat down on the steps with my head in my hands. I felt the surge of sickness coming over me like a tidal wave. I sat there in disbelief at what was happening. I was no longer aware of the rest of my life: that this was a beautiful island in the Aegean Sea; that I had just completed my first film, playing a part that everyone told me was guaranteed to make me a "star"; that my beloved Monica was waiting passionately for my return to Stockholm; that the preceding months had been the healthiest of my entire twenty-six years; that for the first time in my life I felt a sense of *direction* to my meanderings. My brain was void of all thoughts, recognitions, premonitions, save one: that I was violently sick.

Sounds began to fill the air around me. Strange sounds. Animal in nature and eerie in their disembodied, omnipresent quality. They came from far away. In my condition it was ever so faintly that I noticed it was I who was making them. Someone was dying. Slowly and without resistance. I had no control over my situation. The sounds continued, but I couldn't force myself into recognition of the fact that I was making them. Yes, I heard them, yes, they scared me, yes, I knew they came from me. But *no*, I couldn't feel my voice in my throat, my vocal chords vibrating. They just came from the very center of me, they just *came*! Like an orgasm, not of life but of death. Not of ecstasy but of agony.

As I sat on the steps, it was only minutes before I vomited once again. Not in a large volume this time, for I had already been emptied of almost all matter. This time juices, from the stomach and *strong*. (Days later my mouth would still be raw inside from their burning the skin.) When it ended I was at the bottom of the stairs on my hands and knees.

It took minutes for me to get my breath and once again return to some semblance of a cognitive state. Within moments I felt the coming of yet another deathly orgasm. This is it, I thought. Whatever has caused this, I am not going to make it. How bizarre it seemed, for just hours earlier I had been enjoying laughter and a post-meal chat with my European friends. It began to dawn on me how very serious my predicament was. I must get help! My nearest neighbor— Stig's house one hundred yards up the hill—was my only hope.

I started up the hill, going only a few yards before another seizure of regurgitation began. My recollection of the rest of the journey is like a nightmare. Stumbling, crawling, heaving, dry heaving, convulsing, being on my belly, pulling myself forward with my hands, dragging myself, thinking I wouldn't make it.

I can't really remember reaching Stig's house. How I

found the bathroom and *why*, for that matter, is, and always will be, a mystery to me. Instinct, perhaps, or more probably all that human conditioning to relieve ourselves of our excesses *only* in the privacy of the bathroom. The "waste" of our indulgences are always excreted in private. I do remember coming to in the bathroom, however, and for the first time thinking not only that I wasn't going to make it, but not caring. And then wanting to escape into oblivion, to be free of the horror I was being engulfed in. I was way beyond the ability to cry out for help, let alone crawl to one of the bedrooms. At this point, there was nothing left in my stomach to expel except perhaps bits of the membrane itself. The attacks coming up the hill and as I lay on the bathroom floor were more in the form of total muscular convulsions, like a *grand mal* epileptic seizure. To say that I had lost control is the understatement of my life, so naturally I was also lying in my own excrement. There was fecal matter everywhere. Not that I cared, for when you are begging for that final convulsion that will free your soul from the pains of life on this earth, you couldn't care less that you have just shit your pants and spread it generously around your Scandinavian friends' neatly scrubbed privy. I had, in all possible meanings of the phrase, Let Go.

It was now 4:00 A.M. I know, because that's when Michael Piper, the English sculptor friend of Stig and Sun, came downstairs to get a drink and take a piss and found me in my coffin of shit. I was still having convulsions but no longer cared or resisted them. I have a vague recollection of being lifted from the floor by someone very strong. Michael was six-foot-five and, as you may imagine, a lifetime of sculpting marble makes for very strong arms and shoulders. I vaguely remember a taxi-cab ride across the island: being in the back seat, turning corners very fast. Michael and Stig took me to the hospital connected with the mental institution. It is here that I have a very vivid recall of what happened.

I come to. I am lying on my back on a table. An X-ray table, I think, because it has a very hard surface. There are faces circling me. Looking down at me, as if I'm lying on the ground in the middle of a football huddle. Voices, but I can't understand the words. One of the faces is in a doctor's white smock. I'm convulsing. Hands all over my arms and legs trying to hold me flat on the table as I convulse into the fetal position. Crying. Tears rolling down my face. No pain, just my body violently jerking, contorting at will as the ''I'' of me watches from very far away. A puppet manipulated by a puppeteer gone mad. Interesting. Tears. Sadness. A very deep sadness that all this had to happen, that we should all find ourselves having to meet like this. No sense that it mattered. That *anything* mattered. Sadness and tears. Tear ducts: the one orifice that still had something to excrete. Isn't that interesting? And then . . . a needle. Sliding into the arm of God's ultimate creation as it paused in its maniacal epileptic ballet. Then *nothing*. Oblivion.

Nearly twenty-four hours of oblivion, they tell me. I only know that my first moments back among the living are etched in my memory forever. I have not, nor will I ever, forget one iota of that awakening. I will not bore you with all the details, the color of the walls, number of chairs in the room, color of sky and clouds through the window, kind of bed, smell of the sheets, etc. But what *is* important is what I felt upon the instant of rebirth. *Gratitude*! I believe there are very few members of the species homo sapiens who have gratitude. We use the word, claim to understand what it means, and God knows, say ''thank you'' every five minutes of our waking days. But gratitude? *No*. How can we have gratitude when we take everything, including life itself, for granted?! We are taught as children that the world *owes* us! Our parents owe us! Our friends owe us! Our loved ones owe us! Our government owes us! We deserve to be alive simply because we eat, sleep and breathe. And pay taxes.

As I awoke from an abyss that could have been death for

all I knew, *I* had gratitude. I had never felt it prior to this moment in my life. And what a stubborn soul I had been! The infinite order of the universe could have ended it all for me right then and there, smothered in my own shit, and allowed my soul to return again in the guise of another being, perhaps better equipped for the particular demands of my particular soul's journey. That it did not—that God, if you will, did not—has nothing to do with me, with Dirk Benedict, aka Dirk Niewoehner. If anything, it is simply a testament to the strength of my heart, adrenal glands, liver, kidneys. My "intestinal fortitude," for which I can only express gratitude to my mother and father and their mothers and fathers and all the generations that spawned me, and to the specific constitution I inherited.

That's as good as any place to begin thinking about gratitude. Gratitude for having the parents we have. For their allowing us to be born through their union. Not that they are perfect and wonderful, but rather the opposite—that they are imperfect and create difficulties through which we must work if we are to carry the torch of their ancestry into further enlightenment. We must forgive them their love of us that is so crippling and from which we must escape if we are to be our own Selves. We must have gratitude for their lack of understanding that forces us to understand *them* and thereby ourselves. Gratitude that they are poor, creating a condition that forces us to struggle for material gain. Gratitude that they are a burden, so that we can lose our egocentricity and give back to them in return for all they gave when we were infants and at their mercy. Even gratitude that they left us on a doorstep. For those are the really fortunate souls, the ones who must understand the infinite design of the universe if they are to survive in a kindly cruel world that would treat them thus. Orphans without fathers, stranded by mothers . . . how much they share with Jesus Christ himself and his "immaculate conception"!

Without gratitude there is no divinity in our lives. There

is no order in our lives. And we miss all the miraculous assistance that is ours once we are truly grateful for everything. To live effortlessly in this constant state of gratitude is to be truly humble. Not to have humility in the sense of an attribute to be put on, but to reflect absolute humility in our every deed, action, thought and utterance.

That it took such trauma for me to be able to manifest true gratitude was no accident, for there are no such things as accidents. Only our inability to understand the mechanisms at work in our lives. There is a front and a back to everything. My pre-Leros front had been very, very big; so, likewise, was my back. I had taken for twenty-six years. Take, take, take. From my parents, from my college friends, from loved ones, I took and took and took in a very sincere and monomaniacal rush to have a better understanding of myself. I stole shamelessly from every experience, every person I met. I always wanted more information, more knowledge, more understanding, more love. My accumulation was extraordinary, a logical result of my extraordinary appetite for everything.

I took and I held on . . . and then, in Leros, Greece, in 1971 I had my first taste of letting go.

CHAPTER SEVEN

REGURGITATIONAL REFLECTIONS

In 1971, in my Devil's Island Paradise of Leros, Greece, I took my first huge step backwards. Back to the beginning. Of course, at the time I had no idea what was happening. I was merely trying to eat more "naturally." After giving up meat, sugar, chemicals and all refined foods in Stockholm, the fog had been lifting, and I felt so good that I assumed the road to health and happiness was paved with one glorious day of well-being after another . . . the assumption of a dualistic mentality. Good versus evil. Meat is bad. Sugar is bad. Chemicals are *bad, bad, bad!* I wanna be *good, good, good.* So I will just stop eating those evil things.

What an ego! I am always amazed that I did survive. Miss Gloria Swanson had yet to make her entrance into my life with an invitation to dinner. Macrobiotics and a study of the universal principles of yin and yang were months away. I did not yet realize that there is no such thing as "Good versus Bad," that both those qualities are inherent in everything, and that it is our understanding of natural laws that allows us to create balance out of opposites, thereby maintaining harmony, wholeness and health. There is good and bad in all of us, success and failure in all our lives, happiness and sadness in all our experiences. We must learn to appreciate, understand and finally, be grateful for the existence of these complementing antagonisms. The lack of either side of the coin in our life creates spiritual, mental and physical degeneration, and finally the ultimate degeneration: Death.

Those who would tell me during the coming years that I was killing myself were more correct than they realized. I *was* killing myself—my *old* self. Shedding all the lack of understanding, all the excesses that my body had accumulated during its first twenty-six years of life.

During my life, this accumulation took place on many levels. So would the letting go. The sickness I went through in Leros began on a very physical plane, but in the course of a few hours it went from sheer physical torture to emotional, psychological, ideological and finally, a very profound spiritual, suffering. The shit I discharged was not merely the common bathroom variety. In my Kamikaze Cowboy rush to achieve relief, freedom from physical ailments, I had, lo and behold, discovered the ailments of the *total person*. Imagine what a shocker that was to reflect upon in the years following my Greek baptism! I felt joyful to be rid of ten years of arthritic pain, but not so sure about losing twenty-six years of spiritual arthritis. For one thing, I was certain I would lose my ability to act if I was "free" from the pain of my arthritic soul.

It would be many years before I would see most "works of art" (books, poems, plays, music, paintings) as nothing more than the emotional, psychological, intellectual, spiritual discharges of people trying to maintain some semblance of balance and well-being. The "healthier" the artist, the less the "need" to subject the world to his or her "artistic" discharges. The more enlightened, the less the need to write, compose, etc., in order to be able to live with him or herself. The mere act of breathing in and out becomes expression enough of the divine order of life. That we *are* is enough, without the need to "create" art.

This book is itself a reflection of someone incapable of letting go. It is a spiritual defecation, and I will pay a price for subjecting my fellow travelers to its contents. I will be punished, and the beauty is that the hardship of such punishment will allow me to grow, to move on, to let go. The bad reviews, the mockery—the harassment by the intellectual disbelievers who see all this as simplistic drivel from the naive brain of yet another actor who has gone too far out on a limb—will all be mine to digest. For that I am most eternally grateful.

After all, how can I be taken seriously when I say what I know to be true? That what I became at age twenty-six was a result of what I ate for the twenty-six years preceding. What happened to me in Leros was a result of that diet. Not food poisoning, not the flu, not any vicious "germ" out to get me, but a body discharging excess, triggered by the changes I had made in my diet in Stockholm two months prior.

The flesh of animals, high in protein, creates aggressive behavior. It is a food source that provides great energy and, with ongoing ingestion, violent temperament. That I ate a great deal of the flesh of wild animals while growing up in Montana is significant. It is an energy source of an even more extreme nature. Prior to stopping my carnivorous ways I ate meat three times a day. When I stopped, I stopped completely. This was very dangerous, because energy is neither created nor destroyed, and in the case of the body, it is stored.

Eventually, the body will want to rid itself of all the stored animal protein/minerals it no longer needs. The vomiting, the violent convulsions, were all symptoms of a body discharging excess yang, excess animal flesh. In Leros I experienced the awesome power of nature as my body violently regurgitated masses of stored animal food it was no longer required to hang on to, due to my drastic change in diet. Had I known then what I do now, I would have proceeded much more slowly in changing from animal-type protein to vegetable-type protein and avoided the shocking housecleaning my body went through as it attempted to restore balance in perfect accord with the laws that govern the order of the universe.

My body's first reaction to my changes in diet was a

tremendous sense of well-being when it realized it no longer had to deal with the continual bombardment of animal protein, fats and salts, of which it already had more than it could handle. It began to run smoother as the mixture leaned. As I continued to deny my body animal food, eventually it reached the point at which it had to rely on what I *was* eating to function.

What a tremendous change of direction! Not only had I always eaten meat, but all the ancestors in my family tree had been meat eaters. In one summer, let alone one lifetime, I was trying to change thousands of years of eating habits.

It would be seven days after coming to in that Greek hospital before I would ingest anything other than water. And, as in all true processes, there was no willpower involved in this week-long fast. While the Greek doctor and all my friends on the island speculated on just what in the hell had been responsible for them nearly having to notify my mother in the cowboy country of Montana, U.S.A., that her vagabond son had gone the way of the glory that was Greece, I was only happy to be alive. I knew this was as close as I would ever come to being reborn.

From that Lerosian night of old self-regurgitation to this professional moment in the sun of a successful television series, I can draw a straight line. The detachment from worldly things that my father's death taught me was reaffirmed and would eventually be confirmed with the entrance of cancer into my life. My father's demise, my monstrous Grecian discharge and cancer all have one thing in common. They are all the result of a life or lives lived in ignorance of the eternal, infinite laws that govern the universe.

PART TWO

Our life is an apprenticeship to the truth that around every circle another can be drawn; that there is no end in nature, but every end is a beginning; that there is always another dawn risen on mid-noon, and under every deep a lower deep opens.

—Ralph Waldo Emerson

CHAPTER ONE

OH, BABY!

When I returned to Stockholm after my two months in Greece, Monica was waiting for me and the resumption of our star-crossed love affair. In a way that only a woman's instinct is capable of, she sensed I had indeed changed. I seemed detached. Her natural assumption was that I no longer loved her.

In the warmth of the orgasmic afterglow of my first week back in the brisk fall chill of Sweden, she finally accepted that I was indeed fond or fonder of her than before I left for Greece. Which was true! Her "sense" that something was wrong, however, didn't leave her.

She was the first of many women who would react to me in this fashion. It always went without saying. They sensed I was not on the hook. And they know when you are! The female of the species is very apt when it comes to that. They see it in the eyes of the male when he is pinned wiggling to the wall of their feminine trap. They pull a little string, and if they don't get the appropriate reaction, they *know*. They make the male perform, put him through his paces. I was to be no exception.

Well, Monica loved me. She needed me. She couldn't live without me. I wanted her with me, made plans to bring her back to America with me, but though I couldn't voice the thought, it was there . . . *I didn't have to have her in my life.* The more she needed, the more this became true. She was a frosted vanilla milkshake I didn't have to have.

She may have sensed that mutual bondage in the name of

love was no longer for me, but unlike her American contemporaries, she didn't nag. The simple country life in rural Sweden, where she grew up, hadn't liberated her to the point where she no longer knew who, in the final analysis, was in control! She knew.

We said our temporary goodbyes on a cold, gray Nordic morning in mid-November. As I got into a taxi for Stockholm International Airport, a funny thing happened which, had I been more perceptive, should have warned me of what was to come. Our leave-taking had been very gentle, warm, upbeat. Why shouldn't it have been . . . we had decided that Monica would follow me to New York in a month. Just enough time for her to make the required arrangements for a visit to America of (as yet) undetermined length.

I promised to call her immediately upon my arrival in New York. She laughed softly, kissed me, and assured me that each day, each tick of the clock apart, would be painful. As my taxi pulled away from the snowy curb I turned to wave and a jolt went through my nervous system. Painful. I didn't recognize the face of the girl standing on the curb. Same hair, same clothes, but the face . . . distorted beyond recognition. The shape of her mouth, flow of tears, reddish-purple color of her skin, all changed Monica to a point almost past recognition. Almost. I knew it was her. But it would be somewhat longer before I knew what had caused this sobbing dissolution into a mass of total sadness.

The taxi continued on. Unable to comprehend what had just happened, why she could go instantaneously from one condition to an entirely different one, finally, in my male eccentricity, I decided it was simply behavior typical of the female of the species. I was aware that she didn't think I had seen her after getting into the taxi; her emotional letting go was not meant for my eyes. This should have told me something. But I was much too naive in the ways of the universe to get any message other than the one Monica had allowed me to believe. My dream might have enlarged, but my understanding of women had not.

As soon as I got through customs in New York, I went to the bank for twenty dollars in quarters and telephoned my beloved. No answer. She's with her girlfriends, I thought. When I got to Manhattan, I called her again. No answer. She's seeking solace somewhere; the first day is always the toughest. I called the next day. *Disconnected!* Food for thought, that. I wrote letters. No answer. I called mutual friends. They hadn't seen her. No one knew where she was. I wrote more letters. Nothing. I was sure there was a reason. I was right. But it would only be via a miscarriage of eternal justice that I would be allowed knowledge of that reason.

In the interim I got the lead in *Butterflies Are Free*, starring on Broadway with Gloria Swanson. My spies in Stockholm continued to search for Monica. But the fjords were silent. Months passed . . . In May 1972, out of the Scandinavian blue came a note from my Paradise Lost. I say note because it consisted of only a few sentences, the first of which I still remember: "Dirk, I come."

Well, Rhett Butler in all his Southern hospitality and charm had nothing on yours truly. I sent air fare and waited expectantly for her arrival. She came. She was even more beautiful than I remembered. Mr. Ravel played encore upon encore.

It was the time of my life. I was up in lights on Broadway, making more money than I had ever dreamed possible, and I had plans. Plans which included Miss Sweden. Through a judge I had made the acquaintance of, I could arrange for her to get a green card. She would stay in America. Life would be lived. We would have fun.

Rhett would have been proud of me, for I never asked, nor did I demand to know, why in the name of Strindberg she had gone underground on me for seven months. And more to the point, why she had all of a sudden decided to bless me with her passionate presence.

Several days before she was to return to Sweden, she decided to tell me. She loved me "too much" (always an ominous sign). She was fearful that I didn't love her "in the same way." She was afraid of losing her own identity by loving me so much. I seemed distant when it came to really needing her, wanting her, committing to her. My constant philosophizing about my life's dreams made her nervous. She didn't really understand what I wanted! All my talk of being free from this, free from that, letting go of worldly attachments, scared her. So she decided it was too dangerous. She wanted out.

But if she wasn't to have me and my never-ending daydreaming, she would have me *without* the never-ending daydreaming. She would have me and have me *not*. She would take the me of me she so dearly loved and let go of the me of me she felt so threatened by. She would have my *baby*!

Oh, baby! Even I, seeing for the first time who was boss where men and women were concerned, could admire the absolute perfection of her plan. Especially in socialistic Sweden, where the government pays young women to have children. Federalized child support. Government-funded day-care centers. In the most profound meaning of the phrase, I had been had! My expendability had been made most evident!

Monica taught me a lesson that countless women since have re-taught. The female decides! The man may do his courting dance, woo, cavort and strut his macho stuff . . . but it is the woman who decides. She chooses the sperm by which she ignites the creative spark as she procreates her masterpiece. She casts the role of husband according to how much money he makes, how much public acclaim he has, how curly his hair, how blue his eyes, how cute his buttocks, how healthy his sperm. And if she is one woman out of a million, she casts further, according to how *large his dream*.

How evolved, enlightened, how complete his understanding of the universe in which he moves.

Monica's particular set of personal qualities may have made it impossible for her to take the risk of loving me, but she would have my *essence*! But perhaps God in His infinite wisdom, or the order of the universe, if you will, saw an incompatibility that went beyond personalities and life philosophies, for Monica had a miscarriage. It was immediately after the heavenly abortion of our love child that Monica had sent me her little note: "I come."

I may not have known whether I was coming or going, but *she* certainly knew, and clearly, it was in my "coming" that I had significance. Like any male humiliated by the blunt reminder that his lot is no more than that of any good stud in any species of the animal kingdom, I was indignant. Angry that she hadn't let me in on our little procreative drama. "Would it have made any difference?" I didn't know. But at least I would have been aware of what was going on and allowed to make a decision, the consequences of which I would have had to live with and learn from. Ignorance was not bliss. I ranted and raved. She put Ravel on the record player . . . and that was that.

You'd think I never stuck around to see the end of *Gone With the Wind!* What romantic putty we men are in the talented hands of a woman sculpting her niche in the universe. I still didn't get it!

It was mid-June. Monica was to return to Stockholm, get rid of her apartment, pack her things, put her Swedish life in order and return to me in America. (Isn't this getting hysterical?) We were closing *Butterflies* on July 6, and I had an offer to go to Hawaii for two weeks to reprise my role, with Barbara Rush playing my mother, the part Gloria Swanson had in New York. This would give Monica about two weeks to do her thing in Stockholm. We would then go to Hawaii together and later spend some time in Hollywood on our way back to New York, where we would set up house. A friend of mine in New York had a car and offered to drive us to Kennedy Airport.

He waited while I walked Monica to her gate. Shall I tell you what happened or can you guess? We hugged, kissed goodbye with words of how soon we'd be together again, how much we loved each other. I turned to leave. I took several steps and then, just like in all the movies, I glanced back to watch her beautiful figure walk up the boarding plank. You guessed it: fade in Stockholm nine months earlier. Again she was sobbing hysterically. Bingo! This time I recognized her. I recognized *it*! She saw me looking at her, turned and quickly ran up the entryway and into the plane.

If this had been a movie, the audience would have laughed the hero off the screen. Thrown popcorn. How melodramatic! How redundant. No man's that easy. Sorry—I'm afraid we all are. This time my sense of shock was tinged with sadness and disbelief.

Monica, my own Miss Sweden of 1971, has yet to return my phone calls, or answer my letters. I quit calling and writing years ago, but I would like to know how the movie turned out, and whether God was once again on my side. Perhaps she didn't pull the same shenanigans again. She promised she wouldn't. I'll never know. And anyway, "Frankly, my dear, I don't give a damn!"

CHAPTER TWO

COOKING FOR LOVE

I had returned to New York from Stockholm in 1971 with high hopes, and while waiting patiently (foolishly) for my dear Monica to get in touch with me, once again I began to pursue my fledgling career as an actor. I had a good agent. His name was Stark Hesseltine, and what he had done for Robert Redford and Al Pacino he was trying to do for me. It was exciting. But my real excitement, my real focus, lay in other directions.

Since my eye-opening, mind-boggling experiences in Sweden and Greece with regard to diet, I had become what can only be described as a vegetarian. I was searching, and the latest tangent in my search for answers involved Adelle Davis. I read everything she had written. Cover to cover. I began making my own yogurt, my own bread, my own protein drinks. And I read, trying to find some clues as to what was behind my European rebirth. I wanted to *know*. Where do headaches come from, colds, flu, arthritis, acne, falling hair, near-sightedness, impotence . . . all the things I had been the victim of during the past twenty-six years of my life. I wanted to know, and the beginning of an answer lay just around the corner . . . the corner of Fifth Avenue and Seventy-Third Street.

In early December I had had what was to be the final audition for the lead in the Broadway production of *Butterflies Are Free*. Two previous auditions had narrowed it down to three actors, myself and two others. For this, the final audition, we were to read with the star of the production, Gloria Swanson.

Everyone liked my reading of the part, but the producer, Arthur Whitelaw, was concerned that I was too all-American looking, too muscular to be believable as a blind boy trying to make it on his own in the big city without the help of his overprotective mom (played by Miss Swanson). Fortunately for me, Miss Swanson saw no reason why a blind person couldn't come in any size, shape or form. Including red, white and blue American. I got the part.

It was several weeks later that I began in earnest the life-long adventure of being in control of my own health. For it was only a matter of weeks before Miss Swanson invited me home to her place for a meal. Good God, I thought, a woman who can cook! The Queen of Cinema, whose career has spanned the history of motion pictures, is going to *cook* for me!

It was after a performance of the play and nearly midnight before I nestled into a cozy couch in the study of her pala-tial home on the corner of Fifth Avenue and Seventy-third Street. I didn't know what to expect. I had seen her at the theater having between-the-matinee-and-evening-performance meals. The food always seemed magical, mystical, foreign. The secret diet of movie stars who can survive sixty years in this insane business? I wondered. I was intrigued and, given my constant search—my own current up-and-down strug-gle to find a way of eating that would enable me to gain mastery over myself—more than a little curious.

The meal was simplicity itself: corn chowder, the way the Indians made it (sans dairy); rice cakes with miso/tahini spread and sprinkled with thinly sliced scallions; *daikon* (Japanese radishes); pickles with watercress; and a Japanese tea, made from the roasted twigs of a tree, called *bancha*.

I left that evening with a warm glow inside, a pound bag of brown rice (which was to be the first of thousands of pounds of brown rice in my life) and a pamphlet on *macro-biotics*. I was on my own. How much on my own I didn't realize until much later, as the months of this new way of eating became a year, became years—five years, seven, ten years and finally the notion of forever. Forever on one's own. Responsible for one's self: health, sickness, happiness, unhappiness, success, failure.

Here began the fulfillment of the dream to be physically one's own doctor, emotionally one's best and truest friend, intellectually the harbinger of no ideology and spiritually to be *one* with the divine in one's self. Then no physician, psychiatrist, philosopher or preacher is your guru. For you are all these things unto yourself.

I began that night to read the macrobiotic pamphlet Miss Swanson had given me. The next day I combed the city until I found more books on macrobiotics. I read them. I applied what I read. And I *ate*.

I had never been a person of moderation. I was born hungry. So it was a revelation to read in George Ohszawa's *The Book of Judgment* that a large appetite is a sign of a strong constitution. *Food* is *life*. Hungry for food, hungry for life and the continual change such hunger necessitates. Flexibility—physical, emotional, ideological flexibility—is a sure sign of a healthy being. The lack of such flexibility, rigidity (which we all associate with growing older and older until we become the opposite of flexible . . . a stiff), is a sure sign of the loss of health: dis-*ease*.

The *hunger* I was born with. The *curiosity* I had hung on to in spite of the advice of countless teachers, professors, peers. The *key*, by which I could learn from my excesses, had been handed to me by Gloria Swanson, a woman old enough to be my grandmother, yet young enough to play my mother and flexible enough to be my partner on any dance floor anywhere!

As I read more and more about Far Eastern medicine and the unique principles that underlie its application, I began to reflect on the many changes I had gone through in my life and especially my nearly catastrophic demise in Leros. I began my study of yin and yang.

George Ohszawa called it *macrobiotics* (literally, "large life") to give it an English word that would begin to translate the unending ramifications that result from the application of it to one's life. There is an order to the universe and *everything* is a part of that order, no matter how chaotic it may seem to the uncomprehending minds of the unaware. All things, *all things*, are in a state of flux. Nothing is static. Change happens according to certain laws of nature. There are no accidents.

Change, movement, is always in one of two forms: expanding (yin) or contracting (yang). Heat expands, cold contracts. Summer is hot . . . yang; winter is cold . . . yin. Man is yang, woman is yin. Opposites attract. Yin woman attracts yang man. The greater the degree of yin and yang, the greater the attraction. Large yin attracts small yin.

All food has either a preponderance of yin or yang quality. The ingestion of that food and the expanding or contracting energy inherent in it change the quality of the human body digesting it, making it either more yin or more yang in nature.

The extent to which we maintain a balance of yin and yang in ourselves is the same degree to which we have harmony, health and freedom from the symptoms that signal excess. Because we are human and capable of original sin, we constantly fall from grace, but with an understanding of how and why, we are forgiven and can regain balance, harmony and grace.

Shortly after my first supper with Miss Swanson and my exposure to pamphlets on yin and yang principles, the light went on in my brain that *I* was responsible for both my ignorance and my awareness, my sickness and my health. There was nowhere to place the blame but directly on my own being.

We do get what we deserve. In other words, our fortunes or misfortunes are a direct result of the level of our ignorance as we hopefully evolve toward supreme understanding. Until that time, we all, or almost all, suffer in the inferno to which we have been relegated by the level of our ignorance. Ignorance of the natural order of things.

But what has a back of *resonsibility* also has a front of *freedom*. And the bigger the back, the bigger the front. The more responsibility I took for my own life, in sickness and in health, the more personal freedom and joy would be mine, as surely as the day (yang) follows the night (yin). I could have all that I was capable of *dreaming* of without dependency on any guru of any kind. More correctly, I could have *only* what I was capable of dreaming of. I was only limited by the size of my dream.

Well, hell, thought I, I'll settle for that. Who could want other than what they want? It was some years into my twenties before I realized that most people don't *know* what they want. Their dreams are not *their* dreams, but the manufactured dreams of Madison Avenue, which sells them for its masters in big business. All false.

The appeal of yin and yang and pre-Christian understanding of the ways of the universe, as set down in ancient Oriental writings and handed down through countless generations until they would reach even such contemporary Caucasian hands as mine, was intoxicating beyond belief to my soul. In fact, I didn't believe. Not at first.

What I was reading told me that anything was possible, depending on the refinement of one's understanding and the application of certain principles. Anything was possible— and it all began at the beginning. At its most fundamental level, life is physical. It is this fact, this situation, that we all share. As we move into other levels of the human experience, differences begin to arise between one person, one people, one race, one civilization, and another.

But in the beginning is *food.* Go without it for a few hours, let alone a few days, and see how many of Sigmund Freud's theories occupy your thoughts. In fact, see how many thoughts of *any* kind occupy your thinking, other than getting food into the old cake hole.

Well, I could buy that. Being born with an overly active appetite that took immense joy in the eating of any kind of morsel that wasn't, as the saying goes, nailed down, it wasn't hard for me to believe that food was the primary concern of mankind. All else followed. Only governments with food in their bellies have time to engage in forcing their wills on other people.

My disbelief began with the idea that what we become as people, individually and collectively, follows from *food.* As we choose our daily fare, we also choose our life's destiny. *And* the destiny of our descendants.

Now wait a minute here! You mean what I eat is directly resonsible for the path my life is going to take? Physically, emotionally, ideologically, sociologically, spiritually? That's what this book said. And it begins at the beginning, at the base level of the human experience . . . on the physical plane. Well, this was pretty wild stuff!

What you eat, the food you put into your body, dictates the physical condition of that body. This meant that my nagging list of physical maladies was curable! No medical doctor I had ever visited or heard about had ever made that claim. In fact, I could never get a doctor to explain the cause of any of my physical ailments, no matter how minor. And it wasn't for want of my asking.

I had always found it strange that we looked down on primitive witch-doctors for their belief in the spirits that inflict us, their concoctions and invocations to cure their patients, while our own modern, civilized witch-doctors are equally (if not more so) given to "concoctions," "invocations" about "evil" germs that infect us and equally mystical generalities about how these things "just happen"!

Macrobiotics: yin and yang. I couldn't wait to poke holes in the bold claims of these ancient teachings. I began immediately. I had already given up red meat and sugar. I had narrowly escaped the Grim Reaper in Leros, Greece. My arthritis had disappeared. My sexual energy had grown stronger. I had lost some weight. But I had no understanding of *why*.

As I read, I began to understand. And the beauty of it, as far as I was concerned, was that I could do it on my own. In truth, the real point of it is that it *must* be done on your own! You must become your own doctor as well as your own guinea pig. Or patient, if that sounds better to you. Prior to meeting Miss Swanson, I hadn't been eating much grain, only what I found on a menu during an occasional visit to "health-food" restaurants in New York. I was mainly eating fish, dairy foods, flour products and lots of salads. Yogurt had become a favorite and I had taken up the practice of making my own.

After the first feelings of well-being when I stopped eating meat in Sweden, and the spiritual rush as I floated on the ultra-high colonic I experienced in Greece, my physical condition had gradually gone back to what it had been before: the arthritis hadn't returned, but my hair was still falling out; I was having trouble getting out of bed in the morning; I had irresistible cravings for sweets; and I never felt really satiated. My weight had stabilized at around 185 pounds. That was up about ten pounds from Leros, but still about five pounds less than before I quit eating meat.

So, with yin and yang as my compass, I began to clean my cupboards. Out went the eggs, the honey, the yogurt, the raw milk, the Tiger's Milk candy bars, the "natural" ice cream, the fish, the endless kinds of packaged flour products. In came the bags of rice, oats, buckwheat, rye, barley, aduki beans, black beans, komblu, hiziki, nori, miso, tahini, garbanzo beans, tamari, sesame oil, tofu, kale, watercress, cabbage, leeks. I began cooking in earnest.

As in all movements and revolutions, there is a community. Macrobiotics, the study of yin/yang, is no exception. Its center is in Boston, and it is to Boston that hundreds upon hundreds of sick and dying individuals trek for macrobiotic salvation from the infinite variety of their self-inflicted wounds. I never made that trek. There were reasons for that. I never made a conscious decision to avoid Boston and the assistance of people there with a much better understanding of yin and yang than I had, but my instinct was to do it on my own.

I was raised in Montana, where that was the way to do it, and more importantly, my subconscious knew that if this application of yin and yang was to be of any *real* value in my life, it must be at whatever level of understanding I was capable of attaining on my own. I was right. The journey has been much slower as a result of this. I have made many "mistakes" because of my refusal to depend on the better judgment of others, but they have been *my* mistakes, and they have all led to an increase in the depth of my own understanding.

As time went on, I was continually astonished by the number of ailments I had of which I wasn't even aware. You can't know what truly clean air is if you have never lived in an environment in which it exists. You can never know what *true* well-being is if you have never experienced it. All my criteria for being healthy were destroyed, and over the years my definition of the word "healthy" would change many times, as my own condition continually improved.

I also began to glimpse the causes of the many difficulties in my life. First in my physical state, then gradually the connections between the physical and emotional states became clear. I could see how my physical state affected my emotional state. I reflected on my Greek experience: the connection between eating brown rice and the monstrous discharge of animal protein, so violent it was almost more than my body could withstand, became obvious. I saw my hair loss linked to the excessive intake of animal food: the tightening of the scalp due to constriction of the capillaries that provide it with blood. Since my hair fell from the back of my head and not from the forehead (the result of an excess of just the opposite —too much fruit, sugar and other yin extremes), I knew it was caused by the animal protein. I understood why my arthritis had ceased as I quit animal protein, with its huge amounts of calcium and sodium.

And in this gradual movement away from what I had been and toward a new me, I uncovered layer upon layer of past crimes, past eating habits and the multileveled consequences they have had in my life. It didn't take long before I had no more doubts. I believed. I was what I ate. I had always been a reflection of what my ancestors had eaten plus what I had eaten, but now there was a discipline, a *direction* to my eating habits. And I had become aware of the connection.

As I look back on it, I can see that the process was slow, but it went at a speed that I was capable of handling and it built a foundation of understanding that no one could take away from me, one that was free from dependency on any advice from any corner whatsoever. I was curing myself. I was also, almost as often as not, making myself sick. But I read, I cooked, I ate. I suffered the maltreatment at my own hands and reaped the rewards of the small but constant gains in changing the quality of my life.

As much as I could, I kept my grand experiment to myself. Until you've tried it, you can never know what it's like to be your own guinea pig, as you take responsibility for your life in every way. You look to no one for help.

Sore throats, diarrhea, headaches, flu, fever, skin eruptions, nightmares, depression—I had them all in the period from

1972 to 1975. No one knew. I visited no one, professional or laymen, for assitance or empathy. And this changes you. The total self-effacement involved was painful beyond description. But you must understand that it involved no willpower. No self-sacrifice. I had my compass. I knew the way. I understood what was to be done. And with each day there were so many signs of encouragement that it *did work*. That I was on the right path. That I could be *free* at last to live my life on the terms *I* wanted. I didn't need a doctor, a psychiatrist, a friend, a guru—I had plugged into the infinite wisdom of the universe. The rest was up to me.

With my introduction to Miss Swanson and macrobiotics, I had become obsessed. My true dream of complete freedom for the first time seemed to be something that was perhaps attainable. I was free from arthritis, free from sexual anxiety; who knew what lay down the road? A road which I began to sense more every day was paved with what I ate. The people around me all said otherwise. To think that food was the key to health and happiness was the thought of a naive child. More than that, it was wrong! And even more than that, it was dangerous! I hadn't learned, *yet*, to keep my mouth shut and my ideas to myself, a discipline that I was soon to incorporate into my lifestyle and practice religiously (until this book).

Yes, I *was* naive, child-like. Little did my friends understand the profound need I had for the very thing they were so adamantly warning me to avoid—*risk! Danger!* This was all before skydiving and river-rafting and marathon running became the obsessions of a middle-class America desperate to do just that: bring a little risk, a little sense of adventure, into the air-conditioned nightmare of their suburban life. They are people going insane from the lack of risk in their lives.

If they want real danger, real risk, they should forget climbing mountains, jumping from planes, rafting the few remaining wild rivers, and start changing the chemistry of their blood in the laboratories of their kitchens. This involves a thrill that can bring terror to the stoutest of hearts. No parachutes, no ropes, no exotic, expensive paraphernalia, no "experts" to guide you. Just you and your pots taking a journey into the center of your soul. Down the infinite river of your blood stream.

That I will always be grateful to Miss Swanson for inviting me to dinner is an understatement of infinite proportions. The women who have wanted to cook for me I can, to this day, count on one hand. Ski with me, dance with me, walk with me, talk with me, perform any and all manner of love-making with me, yes; but move into a kitchen and create a meal for the two of us to share . . . seldom.

I had the misfortune to be born in that generation when the female of the species was to begin doing what her mother only privately fantasized about . . . getting out of the kitchen! It became a sign of female self-realization *not* to know how to cook. And those teenage girls of the sixties were soon to have the fulfillment of their ultimate dream, the ultimate sign of "liberation": freedom from creating *life*! No more babies.

I constantly meet those "liberated women" of the sixties and seventies, now successful, independent, despairing women plunging through their thirties. Childless, husbandless, they wonder—at a hundred dollars an hour—why they have been cursed with the "biological clock syndrome," why they feel so empty. Why all the men they meet are incapable of any serious commitment. That it all leads back to their inability to cook, their refusal to take charge of the home and the health of a man, kids, a family, is too blatantly simple for them to understand, too insulting for them to accept.

Well, in 1971 *I* began cooking. I was cooking, and all the women I dated, flirted with, was infatuated with, made love with, to, at—they *weren't* cooking. What chance did I have with them?

I was rapidly beginning to think of cooking as an art form. The highest art form. With *food* one creates *life*, and the more profound the creation of that food the more profound the life that flows out of it. How fitting and proper that it should have been a woman, Gloria Swanson, who would trigger this realization.

And so it began, thousands of meals in hundreds of kitchens. Breakfast for one, lunch for one, dinner . . . for one. No longer looking for love, I was now cooking for love.

CHAPTER THREE

PIGSKIN AND GREASEPAINT

John Gielgud once said, "It is important for an actor to always remember the initial reason he decided to become an
actor." How easy it is to forget that in the chaos and confusion that surrounds the building of any career. But I am
very clear on the "why" of my acting dream. My first experience with acting was during my freshman year at Whitman College in Walla Walla, Washington. Fortune would
have it that I would appear on a stage before I ever saw a live
theatrical production! Fortune also smiled (there are no accidents) in that Whitman College had (and has to this day)
the most marvelous Theatre Department.

During my freshman year at Whitman, on a dare I audi-
tioned for the spring musical, *Showboat*. I had sung in the
high-school choir—music was my real love in life—and I was
planning on getting a degree in composition if, indeed, I
managed a degree in anything. So I thought I would impress
my football buddies by going into the "weird" world of
theatrics and singing a couple of tunes. They didn't know
I could carry a tune. Theatre majors were all weirdos anyway, and they were thoroughly impressed that I had the
courage to rub shoulders with their kind, even if only for the
fifteen minutes it would take to do my yodeling bit. I never
expected to win the audition. Hell, I didn't even want to be
in the musical. But I got the part. I got *the* part. The lead.
Gaylord Ravenal, who sings all those wonderful romantic
songs that have made *Showboat* a classic in its genre.

Immediately after the cast list was posted and my buddies

hooted with glee at my misfortune, I tried to get out of it. I explained to the head of the department that I didn't think I was really capable of doing it and that a terrible mistake had been made. He informed me that I was his choice, I *could* do it and what's more, he wasn't going to let me out of it. What the hell, I thought privately, I'll show up, do my best, and he'll find out for himself that I'm in way over my head.

Then a strange thing happened. I found that I *loved* it. I loved the people. I loved the *smell* of the theater. I loved, especially, the process of rehearsal, of make-believe. I may have had my shortcomings in the vocal department, I was certainly too young for the part and my dancing . . . well, it lacked finesse (although it did have enthusiasm), but I did have several qualities that saved the day. Qualities that I much later discovered are in rather limited supply among the rank and file of the Screen Actors' Guild. I was vulnerable and I *listened*!

I didn't have a clue to what I was doing. But I learned the words, believed totally in the moment and listened to what was going on. The rest was done for me. After fifteen years of making a living as an actor, two years in an English training program, broadway shows, films and television, I don't think I have anything to add to that. Learn the words, believe and listen. God does the rest. What came naturally for me those twenty years ago, as a frightened neophyte in the world of thespians, became ever more difficult as I gained experience, got clever and read books on acting, received "advice" and read reviews and *made money*.

I've never understood the multitude of acting schools that exist in Los Angeles and New York and the thousands of eager actors who cram their classrooms hoping to "learn" how to act. All those struggling actors would be much better off to take their acting tuition and bum around the country, or hike through some part of the world. They should have experiences, discover who they are, how they feel, what they think. Learn how to live. Then bring that to the stage and screen.

Instead, they spend all their time by the phone, in acting classes, talking to other actors about acting, talking to agents, meeting for lunch. When they *do* get hired, what have they got to bring to a role? They've been living in a bubble, like hot-house tomatoes; there are no edges, no character. It all blends and bores. The extent to which we are capable of living complete lives is the same extent to which we are capable of giving complete performances.

Ever wonder why animals are so irresistable on the stage? Audiences can't take their eyes off them. Or young children, before they begin to go the way of all adults and start getting clever. Irresistible! Animals and kids. They never make a false move on stage. They are incapable of it. From the bottoms of their feet to the top of their heads, they are connected, totally involved in each moment.

My dad was so right. As a lad in Montana, playing football and basketball on the high-school team was an endeavor that thrilled me, body and soul. But there were those around me who belittled my complete joy and enthusiasm for the weekly games. After all, they reminded me, it was only "high-school" football, and White Sulphur Springs was only a little cow town (pop. 1,000) in the middle of the nowhere that was Montana, and we didn't even have enough students to play eleven-man football. Only a couple of hundred people came to the games, and my friends went on and on with their worldly perspective on the real significance of high-school football and basketball in Montana in the early sixties.

I should wait till I played on a college team, they admonished me. Now *that* was big time! The pros! It was okay for them to be excited about playing—they had something to be excited about: millions of people watched them; magazines put them on their covers; they earned thousands of dollars.

All this cold water had its intended effect. I was beginning to wonder whether there was something wrong with me because I found my athletic career in a small high school in Big Sky country so mind-boggling exciting. Then one Saturday afternoon before the game, my father took me aside and told me something I have never forgotten: "Dirk, if you go on to play football at Ohio State; if the Green Bay Packers draft you number one and you make thousands of dollars and achieve national stardom, it will *never* be better than it is right now, playing eight-man football in this little town in Montana. The *experience* of playing will *never be* more fulfilling."

He was right. I did go on to play football in college, and it *was* never better than on those glorious autumn days in Montana, when the experience was pure and the game was played for the sheer joy of playing. Winning was the goal, of course, but it wasn't everything. The experience was everything, unadulterated by worldly conditioning that something was missing because the world wasn't watching and it wasn't making anybody rich. My father's words have come back to me hundreds of times as I ride the roller coaster that has been my professional career. Oh, how right he was!

How sad it is that most of us miss the moments at hand that, strung together, comprise our lives. I've seen it too many times: singing in a college musical, we wish it were a Broadway musical; when it becomes a Broadway musical, we pine away that it isn't a movie musical; and when it becomes a film, we make ourselves unhappy because we don't have the lead. And even if we *do* get the lead in a musical for 20th Century-Fox, receiving millions of dollars, we still worry that it won't be a success, or if it is, that we will be typecast and never get the kind of parts that keep going to Robert DeNiro. Always wishing we were someplace other than where we are is a disease that afflicts mankind. By removing ourselves from total involvement in what we are doing, what we have been given, we deny our natural growth and progression and the ultimate fulfillment of a destiny that was meant to be ours. *And* we miss all the *fun!*

John Gielgud was right: it is important to remember the initial reaction that prompted an involvement in the intangible world of make-believe. The experience has never been more fulfilling for me than it was in May 1964, on that small college stage in Walla Walla, Washington, as the house lights dimmed and I crooned "Only Make Believe."

In life, as on the stage, if we would only say the words, believe in the moment and listen to the world that is going on constantly all around us. There is opportunity in every breath of fresh air. Let go and enjoy. Get out of the way. The rest is done for us.

CHAPTER FOUR

MISCAST OUTCAST

To this day the fact that I have an acting career I find astonishing. Proof that we get what we deserve, have what we're supposed to have, no matter what plans we make for ourselves. "There's a divinity that shapes our ends, rough-hew them how we will." And oh, that little voice within us that so often tells us to do that which all the world around us is teaching, urging us *not* to do. My life, and certainly my career as an actor, has been a testament to this. The only casting director who ever considered me right for any job has been the Big Casting Director in the Sky. Nothing has ever come easy.

Among one of my earlier rejections was a wonderful role in George Roy Hill's classic film, *Slaughter-House Five*. It was close, but George Roy didn't find me quite "right" for the part; Perry King did the honors. He may not have invited me into his celluloid family, but several months later I was invited to a soirée at his house in Beverly Hills.

At the time, I had just arrived in Hollywood after closing on Broadway in *Butterflies Are Free* and was busy meeting Hollywood's casting agents. They were interested only in knowing the exact beach I had been discovered surfing on. My resumé sat right in front of them, listing countless theatrical productions around the country, two Broadway shows and even a European film, but they just *knew* I'd come back from the beach one day, looked in the mirror and decided I had the stuff of which stars are made!

I ran into George Roy Hill one day at Vince's Gym, where

Strother Martin had taken me as a favor. Strother was a friend of mine and knew I was looking for a place where I could work out. George Roy was there, Strother introduced us and George Roy said he remembered me and invited me to the soirée. I was living in an $80/month one-room pad, driving a 1963 Rambler and cooking my miso and tofu on a hot plate. George Roy's soirée introduced me to Robert Redford, Paul Newman, Robert Shaw and a few other working actors in town. George Roy was kind enough to recognize a man with time on his hands when he saw one and on several other occasions invited me to enjoy his beautiful house and the interesting people therein. He also had a magnificent grand piano. Music had been my passion and I had learned my way around a piano years before. I was desperate for a place where I could get back to playing, so he allowed me to come up to his place and use the piano during the day, while he was at the studio. He was finishing *The Sting* and would later start preparing *The Great Waldo Pepper*. It was great fun to be rubbing shoulders with the mainstream of cinema's best. My own economic and professional situation may have been precarious, but I never missed an invitation to park my beat-up Rambler among the Rolls, Mercedez-Benz's and Porsches in George Roy's driveway.

I wanted to do something for George Roy in appreciation of all the interesting times I'd had as a result of his kindness. I didn't then, and to this day haven't any idea why I was put on the guest list. Pity, perhaps. Or curiosity on George Roy's part. But there I was and I did want to repay him in some fashion. I was going to Montana for Christmas 1973, and while at home I went fishing, as I always do in Montana. I caught a mess of brook trout (through the ice) and brought them back and offered to have a fish dinner at George Roy's place. *I* would bring the main course. What a guy! Fresh trout caught through my own expertise just days before in the frozen beaver ponds on Birch Creek, on my old buddy

Rick Buckingham's ranch. I was impressed. I assumed George Roy would be. At least, I think he appreciated the gesture.

Among the dinner guests was Robert Redford. To this day I remember him on that occasion, and on several others at Hill's place, as the most charming human being I had ever been around. Had it been he instead of me who'd been fishing in Montana, I'm sure he could have simply charmed the fish right onto the hook. I mentioned this to George Roy and said that it was certainly no accident that Redford was a star. He had *it*. The stuff, charisma, charm, whatever you want to call it.

George Roy put it another way, which explained my lack of success with the casting gurus of Hollywood. "You'll never be a star, Dirk," he told me. "You could be a star, but you won't. You don't *want* it badly enough." I wondered if he'd been talking with a certain Swedish girl somewhere in Stocholm and if so, could he give me her number. I let it pass. But I did think about it.

I wanted to work. I was an actor. I wanted to act. But he was right—I *didn't* want to be a movie star. Never had wanted to be a movie star. I was so naive as to assume that anyone who knew me would know that went without saying. I wouldn't *refuse* stardom, recognition, acclaim. I had no axe to grind either way. But didn't George Roy Hill realize that it was precisely the *lack* of craving for what all his other guests had that allowed me to have such a wonderful time in their presence? I wasn't wishing I was somewhere else, somebody else, richer or more famous. I was happy and secure with who I was, what I was and where I was. I didn't have to have what they all had. If my company was pleasant, it was only because of that and the genuine enjoyment it allowed me as a pauper among princes. And on the occasions when I rub shoulders with the famous in my Kamikaze trek through Glitterville, it will *never* be as exciting as those few soirées at George Roy Hill's place twelve years ago.

I learned that the minute I opened my mouth with people in a position to hire me, I confused them. They couldn't get an "angle" on me. Their instincts then, and those of network casting departments later, were right. I wasn't what I appeared to be. I was living my life for stakes much higher than the winning or losing of a part. Jobs, careers, network executives would come and go, but "I" was all I had. The enjoyment of this lifetime was all I had. God had cast me in the only "role" that really mattered, and it was much more complicated, interesting and challenging than any role mankind could create in any cinematic fantasy. I didn't realize it, but I was no longer an actor.

Which is why my career has truly been a miracle and why any success I have had has always been in spite of myself. Ask any of my friends who have been witnesses to my career and they will attest to the awe with which they have seen me survive and function while seeming to remain quite personally detached. God has been my Agent.

Nothing came easy. And then finally nothing came. Period. The fact that my professional career was gradually dying on the vine was no accident either. As my former, *old* self died, so did all the things attached to it. Slowly at first, but after 1975 with ever-increasing rapidity. I am so glad that the films and the TV series I did "B.C." (before cancer) didn't garner me the "stardom" that so many people around me predicted. For that acclaim would have had to vanish also, and it was difficult enough to let go of a career of semi-success.

As my old skin changed, so did my waistline, my sodium/potassium ratio, my pulse and my blood pressure. And so also did every niche of my social world. Friends, professional and personal, let go of me as they unconsciously no longer found me to be what I had been. "You've changed," I heard them say time and again. If they only knew how profoundly correct they were.

The early spring of 1975 found me living in Manhattan Beach, California, sharing a place near the beach with an old friend from my New York days. I hadn't worked in a year, except for a small part in a movie of the week that a friend of mine had arranged to keep me from starving.

Actually, I had always been frugal. My way of eating was, on top of everything else, economical beyond anyone's wildest imaginings. Grain, beans, vegetables. I could eat all I wanted and/or needed for two dollars a day. My friend's concern over my "starving" was a result of his awareness of my lack of gainful employment and the assumption that my cupboard must be bare.

William Morris was my agency and seemed intent on allowing me the opportunity to see just how little I could live on. They were always very kind with encouragement, however, and even in the darkest hours of my unemployment continued to remind me that I could, should and would be a star. They never actually had meetings for me, but I was constantly assured that such an event was just around the corner and that we should have lunch and discuss it.

This was my situation in April of 1975. A situation that was all a result of my own doing. I was getting, as we all do, exactly what I deserved. How long I would have continued on "hold," as William Morris arranged my luncheon schedule, I'll never know. For the merciful order of the universe stepped in and saved me from my own inertia. Dirk Benedict may have been on "hold," but his soul was gnashing at the bit.

Which is why I'm glad my career had never really taken off, for I was having a difficult enough time letting go of it as it was. William Morris was doing all they could to get me to let go, but the old me was very stubborn; it took cancer to finally cut my Hollywood umbilical cord. My journey was about to begin in earnest. Everything changes. I was about to be cast in the most challenging role of my life: Dirk

Benedict, cancer victim. "Victim" may be a bit strong, as it has deathly overtones, but in April of 1975, who knew? It would certainly be one ending or the other. The hero would either live or die. There is no "almost," "halfway" or "in-between." That I knew. This wasn't any Hollywood movie with a damsel in distress and a dragon to slay. This scenario had no girl, and I sensed the dragon to be slain lay within yours truly.

CHAPTER FIVE

OKAY, M.D., I'M READY FOR MY CLOSE-UP

The last time I followed a doctor's advice was in 1969. Since then my only visits have been with regard to my profession, in which it is impossible to get insurance for a film project unless you have a doctor's signature guaranteeing you are healthy enough to fulfill your role in the project.

So in late 1973, when it came time for me to begin filming my first television series, *Chopper One*, I had to visit a doctor to get my seal of approval. I wasn't looking forward to it, although it proved to be more humorous than anything else. During my visit the doctor of course took my blood pressure and pulse. Pulse 39. Blood pressure 103/60. Oh, oh! The doctor asked me if I had been feeling okay recently. I assured him that I felt fine, ran five to ten miles a day, played tennis and if my skin would just clear up I'd be happy as a clam. I knew better than to mention that I was on a "special diet" and maybe that was having some effect on the numbers he found so abnormal.

He gave me one of those benign medical stares, told me to stay where I was (within his grasp) and left the room. When he returned I asked him, "What's up, Doc?" He informed me that my blood pressure was dangerously low, my pulse likewise and that he'd arranged for me to be taken to a hospital.

Red lights zoomed up and down my spinal column! I controlled my instinctive urge to get the hell out of there and off-handedly asked him just how "dangerously low" it was? He told me. I laughed and said, "Oh yeah, that's just about where it always is."

If he only knew that because I was eating grains and vegetable-quality food my metabolism would naturally be lower and slower. Less pressure, slower-beating heart: guarantees of longevity. He should only have known . . . he died just a few years later of a heart attack while playing golf.

Grabbing at straws, I told the doctor I was a runner, that I ran twenty miles a day and was in heavy training, as I hoped to compete in marathon races. Marathons weren't the fashion for the masses then that they are today, and anyone who planned on running them was a maniac!

He bought that! "Oh, you have a runner's heart."

"Yep, Doc, that's it. I'm a real maniac. I wanna get the ol' pulse down to 31 if I can." He warned me to be careful. I could suffer in later years from an enlarged, overdeveloped heart. (Ruin my golf game!) I promised to be careful.

He canceled the emergency-room limo, and I sighed with relief at having survived another encounter with that profession which I had only just recently kicked out of my life.

But it was to be only weeks before I would find myself once again on a collision course with the medical profession.

There's an old saying that goes, "The only two things you can't escape are death and taxes." I disagree. The only two things you can't escape are death and doctors! And if you have enough to do with the latter, you increase your chances of the former. Death and doctors. Iatrogenicide: one of the most startling and well-hidden statistics in America today.

The American Medical Association is very shrewd. They spend millions of dollars each year keeping the nation's attention focused on booze, cigarettes, drugs, smokeless tobacco, industry, lifestyles (stress), etc., so that no one thinks to ask *them* to account for the thousands of people who check into their hospitals throughout the country for cures and check out, bound for the morgue with a tag around their big toe.

As long as you believe in the myth that doctors know anything about health, you are lost. Time is finally beginning to loosen the stranglehold the medical experts have on the people of this country. People are at last beginning to *question their doctors*! After decades of failure, it is mind-boggling that it should take them this long to realize the fallibility of their doctors, but generations of worship at the medical altar is a tough tradition to overcome. Especially when all those generations of faithful followers have allowed themselves, their children and their children's children to forsake their own instincts for the "advice" of their physicians. Never question the doctor!

Have you ever questioned the wisdom of your doctor's advice? If so, you understand the absolute arrogance of the medical profession. The American Medical Association is terrified that there will someday be an uprising, a revolution by the American people . . . that they will begin to *demand answers*. Demand accountability for the billions upon billions of dollars spent to find the cures they never find, while they lead us to believe success is just around the corner . . . all that is needed is "another billion or two."

Medicine is a profession immersed in *failure*, not in success, as they would have you believe. For example, the *New England Medical Journal* recently announced the results of their study on cancer: "The 30-Year War on Cancer, 1956–86, is a 'Qualified' Failure." Cancer in the American public has increased ten percent during this period; certain kinds of cancer have increased even more.

If doctors were successful, they wouldn't all be so rich; there wouldn't be a hospital on every other corner of every city in this country. *If tomorrow every doctor was ordered by the United States Government to stop practicing medicine, the overall health of the general public would improve dramatically!*

Doctors don't cure anybody of anything! They don't cure because they treat symptoms, not causes. They push drugs which create more disease, for which they then create more drugs. *Drugs!* Legal if your family doctor prescribes them; illegal if your son or daughter buys them during lunch period at school. Check the medicine cabinet in your home. What does it look like? A pharmacy?

Legal drugs, illegal drugs, pharmacy or corner peddler . . . what's the difference, and who has decided what's legal and what's illegal? Men have decided. Men who take drugs. In time, marijuana will be legal. Cocaine will be legal. How can they not be when an entire country is using them? Show me a family that is drug-free, illegal or legal, and I'll show you one family in ten million.

My house is drug-free. My medicine cabinet and my kitchen cupboard are one and the same. My food is my medicine. Living drug-free is no easy matter; living doctor-free is next to impossible! Doctors are so tied into the fabric of American society that virtually every venture in this country must eventually come under their auspices. Nothing happens without their blessing. Their very expensive blessing. (Including, to make the point in the extreme, *motherhood.*)

Well, I ain't waiting for M.I.T., A.M.A. or any other institution to give me the go-ahead. It may disturb you to know you can't trust your doctor. I'm sorry—but you either take responsibility for your own health or you continue on with the masses, your head stuck ostrich-like in the collective black bag of modern medicine.

I was in the middle of filming *Chopper One* in February of 1974. I still lived in my eighty-dollar-a-month, one-room pad. It was on Wilshire Blvd., near Beverly Glen. Anyone familiar with Southern California real estate will tell you that no such place exists, not even way back in 1974. Well, it did. It was a little room over a garage in the back of a bunch of apartments which rented for the more fashionable rate of $500 to $600 a month. I discovered the place quite by accident and it fit my needs perfectly.

It was inexpensive, within walking distance of Westwood, where I could people-watch, buy a paper and treat myself to a movie when feeling particularly flush. It had a refrigerator but no stove, so I did all my cooking on a hot plate. To this day I am quite an expert at fixing a three- or four-course meal on a single-burner hot plate.

My little nest and the entire apartment complex to which it was affixed in its bastardly way have long since gone the way of others like them. Torn down to make room for the twenty-story high-rise condominium extravagances that now crowd the boulevard and house the retired wealth of Southern California.

I had been living in this little apartment since November of 1972. It was humble and it was home. I was happy and content with it. When I landed the lead in *Chopper One*, I could, of course, have afforded to move into something more plush. But I desired nothing that my current lodgings didn't already have, so I stayed put . . . against the advice of friends, agents and girlfriends. It proved, once again, to be a very wise decision, for during the coming years of unemployment when I dropped everything to put my prostate back into working order, I lived on the money I had saved during my two-and-a-half-year stay in this eighty-dollar-a-month walk-up.

We did thirteen episodes of *Chopper One*. ABC Television then canceled it. Wisely. Once again the experts were wrong . . . it didn't make me a star. I slipped quietly back into unemployed anonymity. But for those few brief months in early 1974 I was on prime-time national television. All 185 pounds of me. There I was: three years off animal food and struggling to quit sugar as I tried to deal with my first taste of the power of television. It has often occured to me that if I wished, which I don't, I could deny many of my early failures, as the change in my appearance is so total that no one would believe it was the same person. *Only* the name has remained the same. I don't look the same, weigh the same, talk the same, think the same . . . I don't even act the same.

As I continued my macrobiotic journey while filming *Chopper One*, the change in me that was most irritating and disturbing, for fairly obvious reasons, was the continual discharge of animal protein and fat via the pores of my skin, i.e., pimples. Nobody likes to go through a day with four or five festering red sores, in various states of eruption, covering their face. To have your picture taken while in this condition is even more humbling. To have your picture taken for the purpose of being beamed to millions of people all over the world is a torture that most can only imagine. A face full of pimples on the eve of your Junior Prom or your first day on a new job is one thing, but during the entire course of the filming of your first television series is quite another.

I am now grateful to have *Chopper One* as a visual record of my physical condition in 1974, pimples and all, but then it was a very hard cross to bear. And understand, I *knew* that if I would simply quit eating the way I was I would quit discharging the animal protein, and the pimples would disappear. I knew how to stop the discharge, but it also meant stopping my journey toward a distant horizon I yearned to reach. I have had more than several girlfriends over the years who were not only attracted to me but also to the way I ate. But when they began to acquire a face full of pimples, they quickly went right back to their former pimple-free way of eating, not being willing to pay the price of pimples today for no cellulite tomorrow. In some people's cases, the body can store excess for many years before aggravating symptoms begin to manifest themselves, especially if those people are in their twenties.

So I made *Chopper One* and shared my sickness with the world. Such is the nature of my profession. Today, in various countries *The A-Team* and *Chopper One* sometimes run concurrently. Friends of mine who have visited these countries find it hard to believe that it is the same Dirk Benedict in both shows. I tell them the truth: "*It's not* the same person." Only the name has been left unchanged—to protect the guilty who said it couldn't be done.

I had developed a daily routine: I would rise early, around 4:00 A.M., fix a breakfast of miso soup and oatmeal, fix a lunch to take with me, put it in a little knapsack (which I still have to remind me) and jog the three miles to 20th Century-Fox Studios, where the series was being filmed. In the evening I would run the three miles home, take a shower and fix dinner, usually something light like brown rice or buckwheat noodles and vegetables. Not only was I working long hours and eating simple food but I was also getting in six miles a day of running. The work days were long, usually 7:00 A.M. to 7:00 P.M., so I didn't get home until 7:30 or so. Because I was working all day every day, I was free from any temptations to "cheat." The food stayed basic and I was very active. The perfect combination to bring about change.

As the filming continued, and the jogging continued, and my hot plate continued to cook up my daily meals, I was experiencing very strong side-effects. I had yet to understand that the journey never ends, or in other words, that there is no such thing as *perfect health*. One does not arrive at a given point at which all negative factors cease and only positive ones are in effect. I still suffered from my all-American brainwashing that eventually one "graduates," gets a diploma, a gold star, a certificate and final absolution.

In the middle of filming *Chopper One* I became sick. My massive discharge in Greece was still painfully fresh in my memory, so it was with horror that I found myself waking up around 10:00 P.M. one evening with the same queasiness in my stomach. Vaguely nauseous, my only solace was the thought that I lived through it once and I could certainly do it again. Small comfort. Ignorance had been bliss. If we don't know what we are in for, we take it a step at a time and survive, thinking afterwards how grateful we are that we didn't know then what we know now. Well, I knew then what I was in for and I was absolutely correct in my knowledge. Except for one thing: it was a mere shadow of my first experience in Greece three years earlier. I was sick, yes. I was up all night vomiting, yes. I lost control of my bowel movements, yes. But if the first time around had been 10 on a scale of 10, this Hollywood version was a mere 3. I should have known . . . nothing in Southern California is extreme. Not the weather, not the laid-back, mellow, hip mentality of its populace and *not*, in this case, my second discharge of stored-up animal food.

I also knew, as I spent the night retching, that because I wouldn't be able to film the following day and production would have to be halted, I would get a visit from a doctor to guarantee that I was in fact sick. Then the production company could collect on the insurance they carry in case a principal actor gets sick and/or hurt and can't continue working. If production halts, the insurance company picks up the tab. But first, the insurance company must have a *doctor's* signature stating that the sick, hurt or dying actor is truly sick, hurt or dying.

I knew I was sick. I also knew they wouldn't take my word for it. I dreaded the inevitable visit. I was too sick, too weak after a night of vomiting and defecating, to deal with what I correctly feared would be more than a simple confirmation of my physical state of affairs. My worst fear was confirmed . . . he wanted to *help* me. God help me, I thought.

Los Angeles, as we all know, is a show-business town. Oh, there are other industries there, bigger and more important to the GNP, but the real bottom line on Los Angeles' identity, nationally and internationally, is *show business, Hollywood. Everyone* in L.A. is famous. It's only a matter of degree.

Hollywood functions as does the universe's galaxies of stars, each star with its little system of planets circling and basking in its warmth, some closer and hotter, others farther away and not nearly so brightly glowing. Yes, everyone is famous, but their claim to fame is in who they know that is more centrally located in the celebrity solar system than they are. In the center, burning with the dazzle of a thousand suns, are such stars as Carson and Newman and Streisand and Redford. Next to such giants are the Travoltas and Geres and Noltes. And on and on. Then there's television, with its endless galaxy of stars of greater and lesser (and rapidly changing) twinkledom.

And finally there are those thousands upon thousands of lesser souls whose claim to fame comes from how intimately they rub shoulders with any of the more centrally fixed stars in the system. The waitress who serves Warren Beatty his coffee, the gas attendant who pumps Streisand's gas, the car-wash attendant who polishes Brando's wheels, the shoe-repair man who resoles Stallone's Italian loafers, the produce man who saves the best for Cloris Leachman, the dentist who gave Erik Estrada his Clark Gable smile. Their numbers are endless and reach into every profession in this star-bedraggled city of angels. They all have the autographed picture of their source of vicarious stardom nailed to the wall of their repair shop, barber shop, hair salon, restaurant, motel, florist stall.

And yes, my-oh-my, yes, *especially* to the mahogany wall of their attorney's and doctor's office. The only difference with doctors and lawyers is that due to their own healthy sense of self-aggrandizement and indispensability, the grinning celebrity nailed to their high-rent district wall *must* be one of the first magnitude. Like the big-game hunter, they are not satisfied with some lowly rabbit, grouse or squirrel, but must have a moose, a grizzly, an elephant. Thus all who visit these places of business can know immediately how "important" the proprietor is by the size of the trophy grinning on the wall. An intimately autographed perpetuation of the starry-assed superstructure that makes "Hollywood" the wonderful world of make-believe that it is.

In 1974 I was a "star." Not a big one. Just a little nipper faintly twinkling on the edge of prime time, but nonetheless, I was a member of the galaxy. The doctor who received the call from the producers at Fox knew in his Bel-Air bones that this could be a new trophy for his wall. A notch in his Gucci belt. As we all know, the day of the "house call" by a doctor is nearly as extinct in America as the Salem witch hunts. But if you are a "star" in Hollywood, house calls are as easy to get as cocaine during lunchtime at Hollywood High. The address the doctor received, as he readied himself to work magic on some ailing actor, was just what he expected. He saw that I lived on one of the most expensive stretches of real estate in the United States (and indeed, the world): Wilshire Boulevard, between Beverly Glen and Westwood Avenue. My little pad may have been humble, but at least the address was elegant. So the good doctor jumped into his Mercedes and rushed over to get his autographed trophy.

I'll never forget the look on his face as I let him through the little door at the top of the stairs that provided access to my modest one-room haven, perched over the garage of a more affluent dweller in the main complex of the apartment building. His look was one of astonishment, with traces of shock around the edges. Even I, sick as I was, could see what a major *dis*appointment this appointment was for him. No collection of antique and sports cars decorating a four-car garage; no swimming pool, sauna, jacuzzi; no barbecue patio; and certainly no tennis court. To say nothing of the fact that there was no maid, gardener or cook. Until the very last moment before he opened my pathetic little door, he probably held on to the hope that there would at least be a young Hollywood starlet cavorting around with one of my cast-off white shirts barely covering her bottom as she worried her airy head over me, her poor ailing Hollywood door-opener. After all, the doctor knew I was in a TV series and that I was twenty-nine years old and single . . . surely I had to have the prerequisite piece of fluffy arm decoration with which to attend all those celebrity bashes fantasized about by all America.

With his first step into my fifteen-by-twenty apartment, this "doctor to the stars" knew he had been had. I was afraid *I* was going to be. But at least now both the doctor and I had one thing in common: we wanted to get this over with as soon as possible. He, in order to get back to his office and ask the people at Fox whether, in the future, they couldn't give him a little "background" on the actor he was going out of his way to pay a house call to; and I, to get back to resting, which was what nature was telling me I needed immediately if I were to recover enough to resume filming in the two days I had told the producers I thought would be necessary for my convalescence.

With the pained expression of one who is being asked to touch a leper, the doctor approached where I lay on the sofa (you know, the kind that folds into a bed). By this time— around 10:00 A.M. in the morning—all the retching had stopped. I was simply weak beyond words and had a headache that encircled my head completely and throbbed in perfect unison with my heart. Thirty-nine times a minute. (I gave thanks for my slow pulse.)

He asked me what had happened. I told him. He touched my forehead.

"How do you feel?" he asked.

"Weak, tired beyond words, as if I could sleep forever. . . ." Hint, hint.

Fortunately, he too wanted to get this over with. He moved with alacrity into his specialty—passing out drugs.

Without asking me whether I wanted it or not (was I the first to ever question his authority?), he began to prepare a needle.

"What's that?" I asked.

"This will make you sleep."

"I'm not having any trouble sleeping," I told him. The only thing keeping me from blissful sleep was his presence. But I wisely kept that to myself.

The look he gave me as I told him I'd really rather not have that needle slid into my arm was one of total disbelief. I *was* the first ever to say no to a kindly potion of unconsciousness! There was a pause that Chekhov himself would have found lengthy. Finally, with pained, professional forebearance, the doctor set the needle aside and dove quickly back into his beautiful, golden-clasped black bag.

Throughout this little experience I kept glancing at that bag. It was all I could do, in spite of the tremendous test of wills going on between the good doctor and myself, to keep my eyes off it. It was magnificent. The perfect accoutrement to this well-tailored, neatly coiffed practitioner of show-biz witchcraft. It never entered my head that he might even have "dressed" for this occasion. If so, he had most certainly overdressed.

He set several small, round containers of multicolored pills on my coffee table and began to explain the effect of each. I couldn't find the right moment to interrupt him as he gave me his well-rehearsed spiel. Drugs was obviously a field he knew a great deal about. Minutes passed, during which my mind was racing to find the right words to tell him that I didn't want to take any drugs. Then I had the brilliant thought that actually, I didn't have to say anything! He would prescribe, leave the pills for me to take, and depart. I would flush them down the toilet, already well-flushed from the night before, and no one would be the wiser.

But then, to my horror, he rose and went into the little (and I mean little) room that held all the necessary fixtures to qualify as a bathroom. He returned, shaking his head, and gave me a glass of water and three of the little bullets he had pulled from his gorgeous black bag of "miracles." There was to be no escape.

"I'd rather not take them," I said as humbly as I could. Evidently not humbly enough. My refusal to take his prescribed treatment for my condition was the proverbial last straw. "Tirade" is the word that comes to mind in describing the next fifteen minutes.

I remember clearly the theme, if not the exact words, of his incensed monologue. How dare I, a layman who "knew nothing about medicine," question his medical advice. He had spent years studying. He was an *expert*! I knew nothing. What "arrogance" prompted me to risk my own health by refusing his wise assistance? "That's the trouble with you actors . . . " (Oh, oh, I thought, here it comes) "you think that just because you're celebrities, you know everything! Everybody caters to you. You're used to having everything your own way!"

At this point I wanted to use his own words in rebuttal, substituting the word "doctor" for "actor," but he wasn't finished. He was on a roll. I just lay quietly and listened. I began to be a little afraid. Could he cart me off to a hospital? Get the studio involved by saying I refused to follow medical advice and therefore he couldn't sign the necessary insurance forms? I held my breath. He raged on.

"It's no wonder you're sick, living in this place!"

I found his equating humble lodgings with sickness very interesting and wondered how that was listed in Johns Hopkins' catalog of required classes.

There was more to come. He was walking around my little apartment as he lectured, and the door that opened into the three-by-three room that held the sink, cupboards and hot plate caught his eye. He walked in, out of my line of sight. He was in there for a full four or five minutes; I could hear him opening cupboards, banging pots and breathing.

He's out of shape, I thought, if this little tiff is making him breathless.

He came back into my view holding one of my macrobiotic cookbooks. He was definitely the cat who had caught the mouse. Finally he understood. It was all clear to him now. I was one of *those*.

"This quack diet will kill you!" he shouted. "It's no wonder you're sick! You're getting what you deserve!"

I agreed with him there, but for entirely different reasons. Now it was no longer my being an actor that made me think I knew it all; in his view it was now that I was a *health nut*!

"You people, when will you ever learn?" he lectured. "You think that if you eat beans and sprouts you won't get sick."

There aren't any sprouts in there, I thought.

"What makes you think that the people who write these books, people who have no medical education whatsoever, know more than we doctors who have spent years in medical school?"

I was afraid now that he wouldn't sign his name to the necessary papers to get me out of hot water with my studio, which I had put in a possibly very expensive predicament. On the other hand, this was no way to treat a sick and miserable human being, no matter how much he's questioned your omnipotence.

He paused, confident that I had no answer. He was right. Instead, I asked him a question. The same question I had been asking doctors ever since I first discovered at age sixteen that I had arthritis: "Why am I sick? What has made me sick?"

"What do you mean, why are you sick?" he lashed back.

"Well, so far you've said it was because (a) I'm an actor, and (b) I eat beans and sprouts. Is that your final medical opinion, or can you give me something a little more specific?"

"Don't get smart with me!" he raged. "I didn't ask to come here. I came as a favor to the studio, who said they were in a bind and needed immediate assistance. I have better things to do than explain myself to a fanatic such as yourself who lives like this."

"Doctor, will the drugs you prescribed rid me of the cause of my illness?"

"It's too late for that."

"But you haven't told me what *made* me sick," I insisted.

He just stood and looked at me. For the first time since he began his tirade, the room became silent. He was angry; *enraged*. Then, in a heated, slightly hoarse voice that would have made Laurence Olivier jealous, he said, "The medicines will make you *feel better!*"

"But I *do* feel better," I explained. "Last night was a nightmare. If you'd been here last night, I probably would have taken your drugs to escape the agony I was in. Today I'm better. I'm weak, miserable, have a tremendous headache and feel like I never want to eat again . . . but it's better than I felt last night. I don't want to feel any better than nature allows me to as I gradually return to health. I want to let my sickness run its course, forgetting whatever caused it. You don't believe I'm going to die from this, do you?"

"Of course not!"

"Then I'll get well. It's only a matter of time. I appreciate your wanting to spare me the pain I'm in now, but please accept my personal choice to experience that pain. Perhaps it's important for me to do that, for my body to go through it."

He said nothing, but walked over, picked up his gorgeous

black bag, snapped shut the golden clasps and left. I thought it strange that he left the drugs where he had set them on the coffee table. Force of habit, I guess.

I lay down, slept for the rest of two days and returned to work, not fully myself, but strong enough to work and infinitely stronger, not only for letting Mother Nature be my medicine, but for being forced to stand up for what I believed. It made many similar future moments, in all areas of my life, easier to deal with. We must be who we are.

The imposition of one person's will over another's is never to be permitted, not even when, in our opinion, it is for the good of that person. The arrogance, for whatever reasons, that allows one person to assume he has the right to do so is a sickness of the human mental condition just as surely as leukemia is a sickness of the human blood stream. That food is the cause of these diseases is the undying motif of this book.

CHAPTER SIX

DO OR DIE

April 1975. Manhattan Beach, California. Coming from the high mountain country of Montana, I was curious to try living at sea level. So in 1974, about the time my career began to leave me, I moved to the oceanfront community of Manhattan Beach . . . about as close to sea level as one can get without flippers and an aqualung. Manhattan Beach was largely the home of semitransient individuals in their late twenties to mid-forties. Airline stewardesses, pilots, ski instructors during their ''off'' season. A somewhat swinging singles conclave of leisure-oriented folks. Winters in Aspen, summers at the beach playing volleyball. I spent a lot of time reading Michio Kushi, Ohsawa and William Dufty, author of *Sugar Blues* and husband of my old friend, Gloria Swanson. Taking daily runs on the beach and bicycle rides on the strand. Life was buzzing around me in a whirling cacophony of sounds as people played volleyball (Manhattan Beach is considered the volleyball capital of America), danced in the bars and cavorted through one suntanned day after another.

I might as well have been living in the middle of the desert. I may have looked the part of a surfer boy, but nothing was farther from the truth. I was pondering universal issues and my own particular macro-biological journey. Somewhere down the list was ''my career'' and the awareness that it wasn't happening. I felt that it was time to move, take a step in another direction, but found myself immobile. Paralyzed. Caught between the old Dirk Benedict who had made three films and a television series, and the new Dirk Benedict struggling to understand the many changes he was going through since beginning his experiment in dietary alchemy. It's one thing to change your clothes, but try changing your *skin*! So, in this state of paralysis I was cooking my own meals, running on the beach, reading any and all books on food as medicine and writing short stories. I found the writing a release from the millions of thoughts floating through me concerning my life's current predicament.

California is known for its sunny days, and most Californians like to spend those sunny days "at the beach," maintaining that California tan all America envies. They even fill tanning salons during the winter months in order not to lose it.

On this particular April morning, the California sun was *not* shining. I remember vividly how cold, damp and gray it was. There were only a few hearty souls on the beach . . . fishing or jogging. The wind was gusting. I walked the fifty yards from my house to the beach with a cup of steaming hot bancha tea in one hand and a letter from Italy in the other. It was about 10:00 A.M., right after the mailman made his daily delivery, when I first saw the letter with its Italian return address. I was quite excited for a number of reasons.

It proved to be the most astonishing letter I have ever read. After reading it and realizing I had known all along what it was going to say (which in no way detracted from its impact), I poured a cup of freshly simmered bancha tea and took my walk to the beach. As I gazed out upon the chilly gray ocean and watched the surf pound its beginningless, endless tattoo on the always-relenting sand, I was at once immeasurably sad and joyous. The juxtaposition of these two emotions was in itself fascinating to my objective third eye as I realized the wonderful, horrible reality of my situation. I was sad in that I saw how frail all life is, how temporary, how short. And how frightfully wasted by most of mankind in their spiritually near-sighted pursuits. I was joyous as I sensed that finally, once and for all, I was being offered the opportunity to realize my dream of *freedom*. My months of stagnation and paralysis were about to end. I stood looking out over the ocean and the infinity that is its horizon as the words of that letter sunk in.

The letter was from William Dufty and it was telling me what I already knew. Knew in my bones, in my blood, knew in the proof that was my peeing. But my *brain* didn't know it, didn't accept or act on what my body knew. My brain needed Dufty's Italian-post-marked diagnosis.

When a person is on the verge of *knowing*, it doesn't take much for the light to go on in his own mind. When we are told something we are capable of understanding, there is no discussion, conversion, arguing necessary. We simply *hear* the information and recognize it immediately as *truth*.

But when such information is beyond our ability to understand, then *no* amount of coercion or preaching can convince us. It is *beyond* us in every sense of the word. People can tell you for twenty years that you are an alcoholic, and try every trick they know to make you realize you are one, and all those twenty years of advice will be to no avail. But when you have finally come to the verge of accepting it, the slightest, most incidental remark about excessive drinking can make the light go on in your soggy brain and you realize/accept that you indeed *are* an alcoholic.

All I needed to be nudged into awareness was a letter, written by Gloria Swanson Dufty's husband William, mailed in a country six thousand miles away and based on the diagnosis of an Italian doctor whom I had never met. And to top off the magic that is the wonder of the universe, the diagnosis was done not on me directly, of course, for I was frozen in volleyball land, but on a *photograph* taken by a Polaroid SX-70 camera and sent to William Dufty some weeks earlier!

When the man who wrote *Sugar Blues* and translated *You Are All Sanpaku* speaks, one has a tendency to listen. William had been in Italy trading futuristic physiological secrets with one Dr. Dotto. Dotto was a research scientist in the field of medicine who had been deported from the United States when his discoveries became too "far out" for the established scientific community. A sure sign that he was onto something of consequential truth.

Do I think it strange that the human body can be diagnosed long-distance via a Polaroid snapshot? Hell no. Do I expect anyone to agree with me? Not really. Not in this decade, anyway. We're still in the Dark Ages as far as established medicine is concerned.

They're just getting around to the *astonishing discovery* that dairy food *may* not be healthy for everybody; that mental aberrations can be treated with megavitamins; and that too much red meat isn't good for you! Watch out for fat! Beware of oil! Wow! Next thing you know they'll be telling us that after fifty million dollars worth of research, M.I.T. has "discovered" (I love that word as applied to what has been known for centuries) that whole grains prevent cancer!

A book on the Italian, Dr. Dotto, is forthcoming. The explanation of how he can "see" cancer in a prostate 6,000 miles away is beyond the scope of my little book. Besides, and more to the point, it deserves better than my time and understanding permit me at this moment in my life. And *more* to the point, *you* probably wouldn't believe it anyway. The divine pearl that is Dr. Dotto must wait for a more enlightened time.

Dufty's letter on that nippy California morning was the unconscious answer to my silent prayers. I had cancer of the prostate. In earlier correspondence with Dufty, he had requested I send him an SX-70 snapshot of myself. The SX-70 is a photograph that contains *both* the positive and the negative, unlike a regular photo, which is only a positive made from the negative. Since the Polaroid contains both positive and negative, it is in effect *alive*. Changing. Yin and yang captured on film. With the invention of this camera Polaroid managed to do what "primitives" have told us has been going on all the time: enabled us to take a picture of our soul, our aura, our electromagnetic charge.

The human body is a mass of energy in a constant state of movement. Nothing is static. Energy flows according to very specific principles. Kinetic energy. *Ki*, as the Japanese call it. Acupuncture, acupressure, our more crude electro-shock therapy all approach the treatment of the body by ef-fecting change in that energy flow, *Ki*. Our Italian genius, Dr. Dotto, has designed a machine that rearranges this energy flow into a healthy pattern. It affects the DNA and chromo-somes. With his machine he can tell which area of the body is in trouble, where the excesses lie, and then, through the application of magnetic forces, he treats the electrical charge flowing through the body, bringing harmony, balance and health. Because of the positive/negative aspect of the SX-70 snapshot, Dr. Dotto can scan it and tell where and how the subject's aura is disturbed.

I don't expect you to believe any of this. But remember it, and someday you can say you heard it here first. The peo-ple who have been diagnosed and treated (successfully) by Dr. Dotto are numerous and include a past Vatican resident. I sent Dufty my snapshot. Of all the requests I've had for a photo during my life as a half-assed celebrity, this was the only time anyone offered to give me anything in return.

At the time, I mentioned to a television producer friend of mine what I was doing. He was curious and asked if I wouldn't send his SX-70 photo along with mine. I said sure. He got a clean bill of health, except that Dr. Dotto warned him that his snapshot indicated very high quantities of zinc in his body. The producer blanched when he got that diagno-sis . . . he'd been taking doctor-prescribed zinc supplements for a year. He was dazzled by the accuracy of this magical piece of air-mail doctoring. He'd *really* have blanched in be-dazzled astonishment had he been privy to *my* diagnostic news! I had a tumor in my prostate that was extremely large, said Dr. Dotto. It was imperative that I come to Italy immediately. Time was of the essence in treating this condition.

As I've said before, this wasn't altogether news to me. Beginning in 1974, I had been having varying degrees of pain when urinating, and I was in fact in the middle of trying to diagnose the problem from my own understanding of yin and yang and macrobiotic medicine. I had already been through so much pain and ecstacy in my journey from meat and ice cream to brown rice and amasake that the urinary pain was just one more adventure, one more riddle to be solved, as I wound my Kamikaze way toward freedom.

Then, in the fall of 1974, while visiting New York for a few weeks, I had a shocking experience. In the middle of my morning ritual, I noticed the toilet bowl filling up with reddish-brown liquid. It took a split second for it to dawn on me that the source of this discoloration was my own urinary tract. Simultaneously, I was aware of the burning sensation that I had been having far too frequently as I relieved myself of my daily specimen. The addition of blood to the symptom was quite dramatic. You have no idea with what apprehension I approached each visit to the privacy of my bathroom! Would the pain be only slightly unpleasant or the kind that made me grab onto the nearest solid fixture as sweat popped out over my entire body? Pissing was never boring. To this day I have unbound gratitude for the wonderful, pain-free, golden-brown experience I now have in the toilets of my life!

It didn't take many days after the arrival of Dufty's Italian directive for me to pack my bags. It is so sad that the cliché about Hollywood fair-weather friends is absolutely true. When your career is on the downswing, as mine had been for nearly a year, there aren't many people who care whether you leave town or not, let alone whether your piss is filled with pain. There were few I had to call on either account. I did call my agents at William Morris to advise them of the fact that I would be "out of town" for a few months, and could they "hold my calls." "I shall return." I had the feeling that after they hung up they breathed a sigh of relief, or possibly even wondered to themselves, "Who the hell was that?"

You think I'm joking? You'd be surprised how anonymous you can become when your television series has been canceled. Especially in a town built on "acclaim." There's nothing colder in the business than the star of some TV producer's *failure*. No one wants a face around to remind them it didn't work. Yin and yang. The bigger the front, the bigger the back. For every *M.A.S.H.* and Alan Alda, there are hundreds of *Chopper One*'s and Dirk Benedicts. You don't continue to live with your ex-wife or husband in order to remind yourself that the marriage was a disaster, do you? Television series might not go on, but life does, and mine was on Pan-Am coach, excursion, headed for Italy and the magic wand of Dr. Dotto.

The trip included a layover in New York City. I planned to spend a few days in New York, the place of my earlier and happier successes, starring on Broadway. I was intercepted in New York by a telegram from Dufty telling me to stay there and wait for his arrival, which would be in a few days. I knew what he meant. My Kamikaze Cowboy soul knew what was coming the way it had known the "news" his letter would contain. Italy, Dr. Dotto and his aura realignment machine were not the way to go. No, I must cure myself, be my own doctor, my own salvation. The ancient principles of Oriental medicine, 6,000 years old, passed down through countless generations and saved from oblivion by Dr. Sagen Isiduka, George Ohsawa and Michio Kushi, must be understood by *me* and applied to *my* life if I were to have my Infinite Dream, a dream whose immediate obstacle was the possession of a tumor in my prostate.

I had been studying these principles since 1972 and experiencing the results of their truth. I had survived Leros, Greece; now it was time to grab for the brass ring. Do or die. There was no avoiding it.

The only alternative was traditional treatment at the hands of "modern medicine." I didn't like the odds on that battlefield, and besides, I didn't believe in the symptomatic approach of radiation, chemotherapy and surgery. That was merely dealing with the effect—the tumor. I knew that survival and the further realization of my life's dreams, large and small, demanded understanding and treatment of the *cause* of my prostate problem. At this time I had already seen the results of yin/yang application to my dietary life. Arthritis . . . gone, falling hair . . . gone, sexual malfunction . . . gone, skin eruptions . . . nearly gone, massive energy fluctuations . . . gone, headaches . . . gone, moodiness and depression . . . gone. I *did* believe. How could I not?

However, with cancer, the stakes are a bit higher. If your hair keeps falling, life goes on. But if your prostate tumor keeps growing and spreading, life does *not* go on. Do or die. This was definitely going to be an adventure. If you think skydiving, auto racing, rafting, mountain climbing or deal-making is thrilling, you haven't tried curing yourself of the "incurable"!

So, when Dufty arrived and told me that Dr. Dotto was not the answer, that I would somehow have to find the answer myself, nothing he said was a big surprise to me. I felt ready. The previous two years of yin/yang application had been in preparation for this ultimate test. I did have butterflies, but I couldn't wait for the curtain to go up. The plan was simple. But I knew that the execution of the plan would be tremendously complicated and demanding, like the carrying out of any expedition into unknown lands. However, I was ready, willing and, I prayed, able.

The first item on the carcinogenic agenda was a visit to

a full-fledged member of the American Medical Association. As far as I was concerned, this wasn't necessary. I already *knew* the tumor was there. My screaming bathroom follies told me so. The Italian doctor had confirmed it. My past eating habits were proof that it was inevitable: you can't eat meat (deer, elk, beef, lamb, etc.), to say nothing of milk, cheese and eggs, three times a day for twenty-five years and *not* have problems with your prostate! If you, the reader, have been doing so and haven't been so advised by your family doctor, it means only that he hasn't *discovered* it. Yet. If you don't believe me, keep right on ordering the filet mignon and wait. But don't write to me for advice then. I'm not interested in "I-told-you-so's"; this book tells you more than you need to know to deal with it yourself.

My visit to a practitioner of modern medical witchcraft to tell me what I already knew was done for one reason only: documentation. Proof for the disbelievers in my future who would question whether I really had cancer in the first place. Disbelievers like you. At the time I didn't care an iota what anybody thought or would think. My proof would be in my peeing and the continuation of my life. I didn't dream that someday I would return to Hollywood, become successful and be inundated with requests to share my lonely journey through Cancerville. Nor did I ever dream how many thousands would die from what I survived.

The results of my test were positive. Negatively positive. My prostate was definitely not the prostate the doctor's rubber-gloved hand was trained to pronounce "normal." It was extremely enlarged. Extremely painful. "Yes, I have been having pain when I urinate. Yes, I am passing blood . . . and occasionally blood clots," I volunteered, eager to get the full benefit of his expert opinion. I watched his pulse quicken as his face maintained the professional calm his training had taught him to exude when faced with imminent tragedy. It was imperative I be admitted to the hospital immediately, the doctor told me, as he asked his nurse to bring in the necessary forms. He needed to perform a biopsy.

I felt *my* pulse quicken as *I* struggled to exude the calculated calm of a responsible tax-paying citizen who wished to "get another opinion." I thanked God I had chosen acting as a profession instead of carpentry. My performance was succeeding. My calm detachment disturbed him no end. He informed me that no second opinion was necessary to be admitted into a hospital! He assured me that after I was in the hospital there would be quite a number of "second" opinions sought. I didn't doubt that! I also didn't doubt myself. I had gotten what I came for. The trick now was to make, if possible, a fast, graceful exit before being locked away forever, to become a guinea pig for their infinite array of symptomatic techniques, all designed to do to my prostate what I had no desire for it to experience.

Never underestimate the arrogance of the medical fraternity once you have entered into their sanctuary. In the flying community it is an accepted fact that the most difficult people to train to fly an airplane are doctors, with lawyers running a close second! The never-to-be-questioned authority they enjoy while dressed in their white smocks carries right over into the cockpit. If there is one place where arrogance will kill you, it is in the cockpit of an airplane. "There are old pilots and there are bold pilots, but there are no old, bold pilots." Well, I managed my exit from the grasp of this doctor's tentacles, but not without being warned that I was "sealing my own fate!" *Exactly*! I couldn't have said it better! Little did he realize that *that* was all I wanted, to be master of my own destiny.

CHAPTER SEVEN

GOOD BEHAVIOR

The blood in my urine told me my prostate was wacko; the avant-garde Italian scientist said I had a tumor in my prostate and that treatment was paramount; the New York medical doctor told me my prostate was extremely enlarged and that exploratory surgery was mandatory; there remained only one more person I wanted to see before beginning serious self-treatment—Michio Kushi.

I had met Michio Kushi several years prior to 1975 through Gloria Swanson, with whom he had been friends for many years. Kushi was the leading macrobiotic diagnostician in this country. He was (is) based in Boston, where I had visited him several times over the years. Those visits were purely social. From the very beginning the primary appeal of macrobiotics for me was that it was something I could try *by myself.* I had never sought, nor wanted, his help in trying to understand the principles of yin and yang. I knew that one consultation with Kushi would enlighten the many gray areas of my understanding of yin/yang as it applied to my particular journey of self-healing. But I also knew that, although infinitely slower, the only *real* path to personal health and happiness was through my own slow and painful understanding. Besides, for thousands of sick and dying people all over the country, cast out of hospitals with their individual predictions of only months left on this planet, Boston was a last hope, a Mecca. And Michio Kushi was their prophet. He was a man for whom there was never enough time. His consultation was their last chance for what Steve McQueen had dreamed about . . . survival.

My cowboy roots and Kamikaze soul didn't crave Kushi's assistance. In our few meetings over the years, Kushi had understood far better than I what was going on in the boiler-room of my soul's engine. I believe it was music to *his* soul, a realization of his dream, that for once he *not be* considered a necessary part of someone's path towards health and happiness.

The New York doctor had given me documentation for the disbelievers. Michio Kushi would give me documentation for *myself* and those other adventurous souls who would follow in my footsteps, choosing this alternative approach to the self-cure of the incurable.

I wanted Kushi to "see" my condition, to see the before so he could witness the after. My instincts proved to be correct. Now, as he travels the world, he can refer to me as an example of the powerful truth of yin and yang and what it can do for one's life without reliance on outside help. He saw me before I began my anti-cancer regime and he has seen me many times since. But he never saw me *during*. No daily, weekly, monthly, yearly checkups to see how I was doing. How I was doing was entirely up to me.

"Checkups" are for the guinea pigs in hospitals who never know how they are doing, because they are being treated by those who never know how *they* are doing, with methods the *how* and *why* of which they don't understand. Modern medicines are missiles being fired blindly in the dark. Hoping to hit their mark. Doctors try to "cut out" the right amount of the right tissue and hope "they got it all"; irradiating tissue in hopes of killing the right number of the right cells and not too many of the wrong cells. They use chemotherapy in hopes they won't overchemicalize the healthy in trying to chemicalize the sick. Shots in the dark. And these people laugh at primitives and their witch-doctors!

You have to understand yin and yang to know how Michio Kushi understood everything when we met at his home in Brookline, Massachusetts. He understood my sickness and, more importantly, he understood my health, my strengths. In five minutes of serene touching, observation and a few specific questions, Kushi told me what no one needed to know. My tumor was in my prostate and not in my mind, as many today would like to believe. He smiled as if he had just told me the most wonderfully subtle joke. I smiled back. He had. It was going to be a very interesting experience, he said with his eyes. I smiled again.

With a variety of simple observations of my physiognomy, Kushi told me what a hospital would have taken a battery of laboratory tests, hormone assays, enzyme tests, and finally, a needle biopsy, to tell. I won't even insult your intelligence by mentioning the difference in financial cost. We had been sitting on a little church-pew-like bench in the hallway outside his study. As Kushi rose to say goodbye, he said, as if it were an afterthought, "Please go to our little cabin in New Hampshire. That would be very nice. If you have no other plans, please do this. It would make us very happy." He had just offered me what proved to be the most crucial part of my upcoming journey—a place, removed from society's distractions, where I could begin my voyage. I had no other plans and thanked him sincerely while he continued to make me feel it was I who was doing him the favor by taking up residence in his New Hampshire retreat. Such is the way of traditional Oriental people, absolute humility and infinite hospitality.

We shook hands, he looked me profoundly in the eye and admonished, "Good behavior, yes?" Good behavior: there lay the secret to the success or failure of my swollen prostate. I got the message. Good behavior . . . no cheating, whereby the only one who gets cheated is yourself.

Steve McQueen, finally realizing the hopeless futility of modern traditional treatment for his cancer, began looking desperately for alternative approaches. There are many around. The treatments of these alternative methods are as haphazard as traditional medicine, but they do, at least, attempt to treat *cause*, and not, like modern medicine, only *symptoms*.

In Mexico, McQueen found his alternative. His last chance. He had been given certain dietary rules to follow. But literally days prior to his death, he was still having ice cream sneaked into his room, to say nothing of the one day a week he had organized for himself and other patients at this alternative cancer clinic, during which they would eat all the junk food he could arrange to have smuggled in. He named this day of carcinogenic feasting "Junk Day." Not very "good behavior." His reasoning, for those who questioned the wisdom of slurping the frozen dairy delights he had charmed them into bringing him was, "How can it be bad for me, all the hospitals serve it." He should have known better! While ensconced in Cedars-Sinai, he certainly didn't have to worry about having it smuggled in. It's right there on the menu for any dying cancer patient to ask for as "nourishment" for their raging disease. Right up to his Last Supper, Steve was going to have his dish of frozen milk and sugar.

Good behavior. There would be no Junk Days for me in my New Hampshire Cancer Clinic. There would be no Junk Days for the remainder of my days on this planet.

From my meeting with Kushi, it was a direct line to the little house nestled in northeastern New Hampshire. A direct line that included but one stop: a visit to the macrobiotic supermarket Erewhon, where I could purchase the "medicine" I would be needing. Medicine is food is medicine. Because my prostate tumor had been *caused* by dietary habits, it would be *treated* by dietary means. The list of foods I wouldn't be eating was infinitely more popular and recognizable than the list of those I would.

Since 1972 I hadn't consumed meat, poultry, sugar, chocolate, sugar-treated foods or chemicalized foods. To be added to that list of untouchables were: fish and all other seafood;

eggs; all dairy products (including butter); honey; carob; all
flour products (bread, pancakes, cookies); all stimulants, such
as pepper, mustard, curry, mint, peppermint; all alcoholic
beverages; coffee; teas; fruit and fruit juices; all nuts and nut
butters; almost all oils, including unsaturated vegetable oils;
salt and salty foods; and, finally, all vegetables of tropical origin, such as eggplant, tomatoes and potatoes.

What does that leave? Grains, vegetables, beans and bean
products, sea vegetables (seaweeds). *Fifty to sixty percent* of
what I ate was to be *whole grains.* Brown rice and barley as
staples. Occasionally, all other grains: rye, oats, millet, corn,
whole-wheat berries. (Buckwheat was to be avoided, due to
its very yang characteristics.) *Twenty to thirty percent* vegetables. Especially *leafy vegetables*: green, white and yellow,
cooked in various ways. Root vegetables: carrots, daikon,
radish, burdock, lotus, turnips, parsnips. *Round vegetables*:
squashes such as acorn, butternut . . . cabbages and onions.
Five to ten percent soups. Especially miso soup, made from soy-
bean paste with seaweeds such as wakame or kombu added.
Bean soups. *Five to ten percent beans and bean products.* Azuki
beans, lentils, black beans, chickpeas. (Split peas were to be
avoided as being too yin.) Bean products such as natto, tofu,
tempeh. *And finally, five to ten percent sea vegetables:* nori,
kombu, wakame, arame, cooked together with other vegetables, beans or separately as a small side dish.

Beverages were to consist of *water* and *nonstimulating* teas,
such as bancha-twig tea, or teas made from roasted grains or
boiled seaweeds.

All food was to be cooked, including vegetables. No raw
foods, including salads. Methods of cooking were steaming,
boiling or pressure cooking. Sautéing was okay occasionally,
using sesame oil in very small amounts.

Essential to my recovery were *restraint from over-consumption*
of any of these foods, *not eating less than three hours* before going to sleep and *chewing each mouthful until the food became liquid* in the mouth.

One could write a separate chapter on the importance of chewing your food completely. I used to count the number of times I chewed each mouthful. Try it. Better yet, observe some fellow table companion as he more than likely wolfs down his meal with all-American gusto. If the American public were made to chew their meals completely prior to swallowing, many of the chronic ailments they suffer from (acid indigestion, ulcers, constipation) would be greatly reduced. Chewing mixes the food in the mouth with saliva, creating an alkaline solution which prepares the food for the acidic environment of the stomach, its next stop on the journey into your bloodstream. Chewing also stimulates the brain.

The next time you see me on TV in closeup, check out my jawline. The muscles there were not developed in any health club, but from many hundreds of well-masticated meals. And to think Victoria Principal doesn't even *mention* it in her guide to the body beautiful! Even Jane Fonda, in her fanatical pursuit of eternal muscle tone, missed this one.

There are a number of external treatments that are very beneficial and would have helped me immensely had I used them. Their only drawback, as far as my own experience was concerned, is that they required, for the most part, the presence of another person. For an enlarged prostate, a *taro* potato plaster applied for three to four hours to the lower abdomen helps to cure the swelling. Especially when it follows the seven-to ten-minute application of a ginger compress to the same area. One I was able to do on my own. Scrubbing the body with a hot ginger towel promotes better circulation, which is obviously helpful in remedying stagnation in the problem area.

I've told you too much. Much more than Michio Kushi told me as I headed for the hills of New Hampshire, complete with my cargo of brown shopping bags filled with the medicine with which I planned to self-treat my prostate.

CHAPTER EIGHT

YOU AND YOUR FRIENDLY RAPIST

In 1967 at Rochester, Michigan, I took a two-year acting program founded and staffed by English instructors from the Royal Academy of Dramatic Art in London. It was during these years that I was in the last heyday of my meat-eating lifestyle and boozing was a regular part of my weekly ritual. I shared an apartment with another idealistic young kid from New York City. His name was Michael Diamond. Michael and I held numerous "beer blasts" at our modest one-flight walk-up in the sleepy suburban town of Rochester. During one of these bashes in the late fall of 1967, I tried to throw my roommate of two months out of our second-story window. The exact reason for my action I can't recall. Michael may recall, as he is often quick to tell this and other tales of my wildly erratic behavior whenever he happens to hear any present acquaintance comment on my currently serene approach to life. It wasn't always thus, he likes to inform them.

Fortunately, I didn't manage my drunken defenestration of Michael. In fact, we became best friends. Through the years he has been witness to my gradual change from Montana beef-eater to Japanese rice-chewer. In the way of true friendship, he has judged me not.

So, in April of 1975 it was Michael whom I asked to drive me from Boston to the little cabin in the New Hampshire woods where I planned to shrink my prostate tumor into oblivion. He had to borrow his parents' big Buick to hold all the food/medicine I had acquired for the beginning of my treatment. William Dufty was in Boston at the time, hiding out from the publishers of his forthcoming book, *Sugar Blues*, and joined us for the jaunt north.

When we arrived at the cabin, it was early evening. It was hot and humid, inordinately so for that time of year in New Hampshire. William fixed dinner. Brown rice and a few steamed vegetables. Simple, but delicious. Welcome comfort to the hungry mouths of those who had spent all day traveling. It was after dinner that I had my first reminder of why I was there in this little cabin, five miles from the nearest phone, for it was after dinner that I wanted something that was not available and not permissable for someone curing himself of prostate trouble. *Coffee!*

The quality and quantity of our cravings are for very definite reasons. How many of you or your friends suffer from cravings? How many times during the course of your daily existence do you wrestle with the overpowering desire to have a bag of M & M's, a chocolate candy bar, a cup of coffee, a shot of scotch, a bottle of scotch, a sugar-frosted donut, any kind of donut, a croissant, a diet Tab, a chocolate mousse, maple swirl ice cream, vanilla ice cream, lots of ice cream, a chocolate-chip cookie, a Big Mac hamburger, a cheese omelette, a nice big juicy hunk of red meat, a bottle of that guilt-free "low-calorie" white wine?

Or are you hooked on the really *good stuff* . . . marijuana, cocaine, heroin? Is it a roller-coaster ride you could do without?

How many of you have shared the dream of this Kamikaze Cowboy to be free of all such cravings? Could it possibly be that this paragon of nature, this quintessential creation of God who has walked the moon, built the pyramids, discovered nuclear energy, is a slave to a dish of ice cream? With or without chocolate fudge on top? Don't you find this comical incongruity frightening?

Cravings are *not* accidental or whimsical. They are chemical. The fact that you can't get through your day without a dish of ice cream is not a reflection of a lack of willpower on your part. Willpower has nothing to do with it. Next time you hear a convicted, repentant rapist say "he can't help himself, can't control his overpowering urges," perhaps you'd better listen. There is no power on earth, will or otherwise, strong enough to restrain him. Except the electric chair, and that's a bit late, a cure that treats only the symptoms, but has nothing to do with the *cause*. Exactly what chemotherapy is to a victim of liver cancer.

It may be a bit repugnant to consider the idea that you and your inability to control your nightly scoop of ice cream are no different from the compulsive rapist and his inability to control his overpowering urge to violate, but it is the *truth*. The man who can't control his desire to rape is no more guilty of his crime than you are of yours.

Rape is a discharge, a release from the incredible imbalance that exists in a person. The sex drive gone mad. In the aftermath the rapist feels relief from a terrible pressure (craving) and remorse at having given in to it; he prays he will have the willpower to resist it when it returns. The ice-cream junkie feels the same relief, the same guilt, the same determination not to "give in" the next time the urge overcomes him. All to no avail. Thus, a craving, no matter what it is for, is as omnipotent as the ocean, or the river wending its way to the ocean. They all have the power of the universe behind them. Willpower is man's arrogant fantasy about himself that he can *control* the laws of nature, the power of the universe. How silly. How sad.

What causes cravings? The body craves what it needs to maintain life. In the body there is a balance of mineral, protein, carbohydrate and water that it must maintain to go on functioning. The ratio is roughly seven to one. For every part mineral, the body will crave seven parts protein; for every part protein, seven parts carbohydrate; and for every part carbohydrate, seven parts water. So the human body is mostly made up of liquid.

When we eat protein, we *must* eat seven times that amount of carbohydrate in one form or another. And for every part of carbohydrate ingested to balance that protein intake, we must consume seven times that amount in liquid! What we eat dictates what we eat dictates what we eat.

If you are a heavy meat-eater, you will crave carbohydrates. And when bread can no longer satisfy this craving, the body will demand even more extreme sources, such as sugar, alcohol or drugs to effect a balance in the blood stream for the extreme yang condition that excessive meat-eating creates. When one ceases this excessive intake of animal-quality protein, as I did in Stockholm, there is a qualitative change in the cravings one experiences.

As night follows day, so too will sugar follow meat. Your "sweet tooth" is not the result of a lack of excitement in your social life, or never having been loved by your parents, or a mere quirk of nature for which you must pay a guilt-ridden lifetime of self-denial. That dish of ice cream or box of chocolate-chip cookies staring you in the face during your midnight raid on the fridge is the inescapable dessert to the Big Mac, Kentucky Colonel or omelette you had hours earlier, days earlier, months earlier, *lifetimes* earlier. What we eat dictates what we eat. It's a vicious cycle.

But you *can* change! Change to a way of eating in which you can have as much as you want of whatever you want and still maintain health and happiness. Change to a life of more subtle cravings in which there is no accumulation of excess because there is no excess to accumulate! And therefore, no necessity for the discharge of such excesses via runny noses, headaches, body odor, oily skin, pimples, boils, warts, cellulite, temper tantrums, anxiety, worry, rape, etc., etc. No need for the body to find places to store your excesses as your thighs thicken, your butt sags, your belly bulges, your chins quadruple, your nose grows and your arteries harden! No need for cosmetic surgery. No need to buy a book like this. A lifetime of *freedom* in which the body beautiful hums along, involved in more profound activities than counting calories and reading diet books.

Let's all clean up our acts. Let's all clean up our blood streams. Let's all realize the true source of our cravings: *food*. You never know how dependent you are on something until you're forced to live without it. Coffee, for instance. I wasn't a heavy coffee-drinker at the time and, in fact, had quit drinking it for months at various times in the years since my experience in Leros, Greece. Nevertheless, I would have done anything, signed away the life of my first-born, if I could only have had just one sip of rich, black, aromatic, caffeine-laden *coffee*. But it was not to be had! The craving became so great I could no longer engage in post-dinner conversation. Bill sensed my growing irritability. He said nothing but he *did* something.

I didn't realize it, but I was craving something of a yin nature to satisfy the very yang condition I was in as a result of everything that had been part of my day. Travelling creates yang; the weather was hot (yang); the anticipation and anxiety over beginning my sabbatical was very yangizing; not eating all day made me very yang; the fact that the evening meal was so simple made it even more yang (simplicity is yang, complexity is yin). All these conditions contributed to making my physiological situation at that particular time very yang.

Coffee is extremely yin. I wanted it. Bad. Bill understood. All I knew was I was anxious, nervous, craving coffee, feeling put-upon, dissatisfied and victimized. Sound familiar to anyone?

Watch people. Ever observe anyone capable of stillness? We are a people with wrecked nervous systems, constantly in a state of twitching, scratching and jerking. No one can sit *still* anymore. *Excess of extreme yin or yang* (meat and sugar) is the cause. People sitting at tables may appear still, but if you look underneath the table you see feet twitching in a perpetual attempt to rid themselves of (discharge) their excess.

Balanced (healthy) beings can sit or stand *still* for hours.

Dogs do it, birds do it, even monkeys at the zoo do it . . . we can't do it, we can't sit still. *Stillness* . . . a lost state of grace. Any old movie star worth his SAG card sooner or later came to understand the power of stillness in front of the camera. Stand still . . . it is magic, charismatic, and not even the most clever, maniacal, cute gyrations can compete with it. Gary Cooper may have managed it for thirty seconds at a time in front of the camera, but how well he, or any of the other stars, carried it over into real life is another question.

Daikon was my savior that first evening in the New Hampshire woods. Originating in Japan, daikon is a member of the radish family. It is the shape of a very large carrot and white in color. It is tremendously effective in melting away the stored animal fat in the body. Any woman interested in ridding herself of cellulite should include the daily ingestion of daikon in her meat-free, dairy-free diet. That is why it was one of the vegetables I took with me to begin my cancer-cure camping spree.

Bill boiled a large piece of the daikon, cut it into thin diagonal slices, put a drop of tamari sauce on each slice and put it in the refrigerator to cool. The finished product did the trick. It relaxed me, satiated my craving, and unlike coffee (or ice cream and other sugar-laden desserts), there was no negative downside after the first moments of satisfaction.

There will always be appetizers, main courses and desserts. The question is and always will be one of quality and not quantity. Throughout the years I have come to believe that one should *change the main course* and let dessert, side dishes, etc., take care of themselves.

CHAPTER NINE

THE GARDEN OF EDEN REVISITED

Bill Dufty and Michael Diamond stayed for a few days and then left to rejoin civilization. I was on my own. Alone.

My cabin had no telephone. No television. No radio. I took no books with me. I brought a typewriter and some paper. There were five rooms: a kitchen, living room, bedroom and bathroom downstairs. Another bedroom upstairs. I put my typewriter on a table in the downstairs bedroom. I slept upstairs except on the days when I was too weak to climb the one flight of stairs, and then I slept wherever sleep overcame me.

Although I can't take any credit—I simply forgot—it was sheer genius not to have brought reading material. It was the one escape to which I could and would have resorted as days passed and the utter aloneness of my situation began to register. As it was, there *was* no escape. No car, no neighbors, nobody to have conversations with in yet another attempt to escape from the pristine state of Edenhood. Unconsciously, I had prepared the perfect trap in which to catch and hold my *soul*.

Kushi's cabin was in the northeast part of New Hampshire. I found its immediate surroundings amusing and profoundly appropriate, as I gradually realized what they were.

During the real-estate boom of the early seventies, some developer began what was to be a very exclusive housing colony of approximately a hundred home sites nestled around a little New Hampshire pond called Loch Lake. The lake was about one mile long and perhaps a half-mile wide. It possessed the kind of gentle beauty that is common to that part of New

England. Henry David Thoreau country. Very unlike the still wild, outsized vastness of Montana. No infinite horizons in the distance, no mountains towering everywhere you look. As if Mother Nature painted here in miniature and in my native Montana with brush strokes that never seemed to end.

This little piece of countryside, which was one developer's fantasy of high-income exclusiveness, was to be my world for the coming weeks of self-cure, self-denial, self-discovery, self-realization and ultimately self-rebirth. I began hoping to save my prostate (or balls, to be more accurate) and very soon realized that it (they) were merely the procreative appendage to the real entity at issue.

What better environment than a modern-day ghost town? The development had gone bust. All that ever "developed" was the club house, on the opposite shore of the lake from where my little cabin stood, and four or five other very modest homes, plus a criss-crossing of roads with most impressive, elegant names awaiting the Cadillac traffic that never came. What *did* come were several retired couples who bought early, hoping to beat the booming rush, and me . . . a failed Hollywood TV pin-up launching his Kamikaze sojourn.

It was called Loch Lake Colony. How perfectly it reflected my own predicament! The American Way of Life gone kaput! A colony with no colonists. A party to which nobody came. Perfection on paper, disaster in practice. The "American dream." The final and inevitable result of lives based on the profit motive. How many times, as I walked those early empty streets, surrounded by nothing but New Hampshire greenery, did my mind recall my stroll four years earlier through the Acropolis of ancient Greece. Gravestone of another failed civilization. And the Coliseum in Rome is yet another monument to man's inability to effect peace and harmony in this lifetime. Loch Lake Colony was my glimpse into America's future. My fast forward on the planetary cassette that could be mankind's last chance to record *universal harmonies* rather than discordant nationalistic anthems blaring blind faith in *dualistic thinking*. Damn the blood pressure, please pass the beefsteak; damn the diabetes, please pass the sugar; damn the prostate, please pass the ice cream! Damn the Russians, full speed ahead!

Loch Lake Colony was my second visit to the Garden of Eden. But this time, at the age of thirty, I went all the way back. And began at the beginning.

Time and again I have started to write of my retreat in Kushi's cabin in New Hampshire. Each time I have found it impossible. I am overcome with a paralysis of the subconscious. I can relate all the steps up to my arrival and the departure of Bill Dufty and Michael Diamond, leaving me alone. And I find no difficulty in picking up the narrative after I came out of the retreat.

I understand why it is so difficult to tap into my subconscious with regard to those few weeks all alone in that little cabin in the forgotten colony of Loch Lake. I understand . . . but my fingers remain frozen on the typewriter keys when I want to let it out onto paper. There is an intuitive refusal to share the infinitely intimate realizations, sensations of self that were mine for those six weeks. Perhaps it is simply that such communication via the written word goes far beyond my paltry, inexperienced capabilities to relate something so incredibly primal.

Or is it that deep within, in the foundry of our soul where the molten lava of our dreams is forged into the superstructure that becomes our personality, there is a place that is the source of all creativity; a place that, by its very nature, is without end and without beginning, a place distinct and separate from whatever personality it occupies. A place that cannot, must not, be touched by the outside material world.

I am profoundly aware that I "changed" in New Hampshire. I was no longer familiar with much of what filled my thoughts. Today it is a struggle to remember the person I once was. For today I am, more than ever, the human being I dreamed of being. Dreamed of being all the way back, back into the womb.

All aspects of my daily existence had begun to gradually fall into place. Life didn't become easy, problems didn't disappear, the struggle continued to be a part of living; but I now struggled and suffered and *lived* with a total feeling of harmony with myself. Of being *who* I was meant to be, *where* I was meant to be, doing *what* I was meant to do. I finally became *myself*.

The change was subtle and slow in the beginning. But with each month, each year that followed my experience in New Hampshire, my "new" personality became more self-evident, stronger. I can trace the beginning of this straight back to June of 1975 in New Hampshire. Because that is the precise point in my chronological life when I began in earnest to change the quality of my blood stream according to the universal laws of nature. And the compass for this change of direction from *de*generation toward *re*generation was macrobiotics and the application of yin and yang.

My routine was simple. Oatmeal and light miso soup with wakame for breakfast. Lunch was nothing or some leftovers from dinner the night before and several mugs of bancha tea. Dinner was brown rice cooked in a heavy iron pot I had bought just for my stay (and which I still have sitting in the kitchen of my Montana lakeside bungalow), lightly sautéed vegetables, and either aduki beans or black beans cooked long and slowly, with various kinds of seaweed added. I had steamed daikon for dessert as long as the supply lasted.

During my first days, while my friend Bill Dufty was still there helping me ease into my regime, he applied ginger compresses externally to my prostate region. After all, what are friends for? After Bill left, I soon stopped using the ginger compresses due to the difficulty of managing the feat alone.

Very soon my supply of vegetables ran out, so I began pulling any green thing from the surrounding woods that looked the least bit edible. Trial and error led me to some very tasty tidbits! And some very nasty ones. As I knew the name of nothing I was experimenting with, it is impossible for me to share with you which ones I did find edible. Except one . . . the dandelion.

They grew prolifically along the roads of the colony in the hard, dry dirt they seem to do best in. They were difficult to pull from the ground without breaking the root, which is what I was after in the beginning. So I concocted a tool with which I could loosen the soil around them and pull out the plant, root and all. I can't tell you how delicious they were. So I won't. I still eat them when I'm in Montana and want to remember what a real honest-to-goodness *wild* vegetable tastes like. Delicious. You cut off the green tops and wash the roots very thoroughly. If you want, you can cut off the hairlike roots growing on the main stem. I gradually took to leaving them on, as I found they cooked away for the most part. Then I simply sautéed them in sesame oil until they turned the color of a well-done french fry. In time I eventually got around to trying the dandelion greens, too. I would steam them lightly and found them delicious. But if you try it, make sure the leaves are from a young plant.

A fantastic thing happened when I was left alone in New Hampshire: I stopped *thinking*. I began to enter into a continual state of meditation, while at the same time eating the simple diet I have previously described as treatment for my prostate. In other words, for all intents and purposes, I spent my days in *prayer* (meditation) and *fasting*!

For centuries people have argued over the significance of Jesus Christ's alleged ability to perform miracles: to heal the sick . . . cure the blind . . . make the lame walk. Did He perform such miracles or didn't He? And if so, *how*? What did Jesus Christ recommend for all His disciples? Prayer and fasting. Did He actually perform his "miracles"? Of course. But to Him, and to any who understand and live according to the divine laws of nature, they were not miracles. You can do it, I can do it. I *did* it. I performed a "miracle." Prayer and fasting . . . eating according to divine principles founded in laws that govern infinity itself.

Have you ever been obese and lost weight? Have you ever recovered from alcoholism? Have you ever quit an ice-cream addiction? Have you ever quit any routine of excess? If so, you can begin to appreciate the sensation I had in New Hampshire: the growing *clarity* and *lightness* that seeped into every fragment of my being. Layer upon layer of fog lifted from my senses.

I would walk for hours along the deserted roads of the undeveloped development. I discovered patches of wild strawberries. I would get down on my hands and knees and smell them. Touch them. But I never picked one of all the thousands I discovered. They were not for me.

For the first time I began to see *all* food as a living thing. A vibration. I saw the strawberries as an integral, necessary part of that little patch of wilderness, and that little patch of wilderness (saved by the bankruptcy of greedy developers) as an integral, necessary part of a larger wilderness, and on and on, with all living things connected in a spiral fashion to one another in interdependent, ever-changing profundity. And if I plucked that one strawberry, it would have to be out of an intuitive need to maintain my own harmony. Anything else would be excessive and a crime against this vast design of which we all, strawberries and people, are an infinitesimal part.

This made me reflect upon another patch of wilderness in another part of the forest during another time. The apple that

Eve proffered Adam can only be seen in perspective by someone who has gone without anything sweeter than a raw carrot for a good long time. Those strawberries I admired on
all fours might not have gone uneaten had they been dangled
from the dainty fingers of an unclothed virgin.

Man's craving for sweets has always been his downfall.
The satisfaction of this need drives him to greater and greater
extremes as it takes him farther out on the sensorial limb. As
the fructose in Adam's apple hit his blood stream and his
blood-sugar count skyrocketed, you can bet he'd never had
a high like that before! And with this *knowledge* began the
search that taste buds have carried on through the centuries,
lusting for ever more powerful rushes of main-line nirvana.
What one apple did for Adam, and white suger did for six-
teenth-century European royalty, cocaine does for contemporary American society. And if that isn't a fall from grace,
then God didn't make little green apples and it don't rain in
Loch Lake Colony in the springtime!

The trick is to get *back* to the Garden of Eden, back to a
reality in which your taste buds recognize *truth* when they
taste it, back to the complex carbohydrates of whole grains
and the steady flow of peace and harmony in your veins. So
when your loved one offers you a Winchell's donut or a
triple-decker ice-cream cone or a line of coke, you would do
well to consider the source and question the motive.

"I've never felt better in my life" is what we all tell one
another upon entering into some new routine of disciplinary
action aimed at getting our act together. Well, I *had* never
felt better, and then it began to go beyond feeling better or
worse. I had never felt like this at all!

When I began my stay in New Hampshire, I was naturally very much aware of why I was there. I had a tumor of
the prostate. I was going to cure myself by not eating certain foods. It would take time, but I believed in the principles

at work and I was determined to do it. I also had no doubt. I believed. It wasn't long, however, before I gave no thought as to whether my tumor was dissolving or not. The experience itself was becoming such a totally new, unbelievable journey that each day was a wonder of new vibrations, sights and smells.

I hadn't been there very long when, late one afternoon, it began to rain. A late spring rain of incredibly soft, warm drops. I took off my clothes and walked out into it. My intention was to stand briefly outside and return once again to the dryness within. I just wanted to see what it was like. It felt *divine*. It was in that moment, standing in the rain, that this book became an inevitability. I have yet to come back in from that heavenly shower.

As I stood there and the rain fell on me, washing me farther and farther into myself, I was overwhelmed by the utter simplicity of living. And it is to this precise moment that I trace the beginning of my life: the realization of all my true dreams. My own raindrops intermingled with those from a much higher source as I mourned the end of what had been *me* and rejoiced in the beginning of what was to come.

For a long time I walked in the falling rain. As I walked, I considered all that had come to me during those first few moments standing in the falling moisture. I would be returning to Hollywood! Prior to this, I believed I was through with acting and certainly through with any struggle to become a "success" in the film industry. It was not for me. I didn't want to be a "star." I didn't want to be "rich." So what was the point of being involved in a profession in which the entire goal is to be "rich and famous"? I still didn't know. But I was going back. Back to finish the cycle. It didn't matter what I knew, how much I understood. It was what I was supposed to do.

Of course I didn't want to return. I didn't want to go back into a business, a community that I didn't understand

and in which I seemed to have no ability to function. I was no good at the *business* of being an actor. Standing there in the rain, I realized the immense sadness this was going to cause those closest to me. Those who had known and loved the "old" Dirk Benedict most. It was going to be a painful journey as lovers, friends and family, each in their own time and fashion, discovered the extent to which I had changed. Some would accept it and continue to be in my life; others would reject it and become mere shadows in my past. Pictures in misplaced, dusty scrapbooks. And some would continue (as they do) to refuse to acknowledge who I had become and insist on relating to me as if it were still 1974. (They speak to a ghost, fearful or incapable of accepting the reality of change.) The essence of what I realized soaked in like the rain: that I must stop interfering with my destiny. I must stop thinking and begin to *eat, live* and *act* according to my divine intuition.

There is a unique point to all our lives, a divine purpose that can only be realized when we get our glorious personalities, wills, intellects, out of the way and let nature take its course. But before any of this can happen, and happen effortlessly, we must eat the food that is meant to be ours as a result of our place in the "Kingdom of Heaven on earth." Then we can all take our walk in the rain. A heavenly baptism in the purest sense.

PART THREE

Man is anomaly incarnate. A carnivore and predator with eyes forward, like cobra and tiger, he inveighs against war and prates about peace. Without possessions, a weakling in no respect self-sufficient, his very survival requires exploitation, but the word itself, thus bluntly put, he finds repellent.

Of all earth's creatures, perhaps only man can think in the abstract, and in the boundless horizons of his mind the universe is but a challenge and even infinity may have an end. Yet this ineffable jewel, born mysteriously in but a few soggy ounces of the body's most friable tissue, ordinarily devotes itself to stupidity and cruelty ranging from ludicrous dishonesty to vices so sordid as to be within the sole province of the human race. No beast can match the bestiality of man.

For thousands of years man has been eulogizing liberty. He has talked as though he understood what freedom is. As though he wanted to be free. As though he deserved to be free. As though he had been free, or was free, or could make himself free. As though freedom was something of which he had always been deprived by someone else, against his will. As though freedom, once attained, would be something he could have earned or dearly bought, and would be something he would forever love and fiercely keep.

Is all of this true? If not, is any part of it true? Or could all of it be pretense and self-deceit?

Freedom! Liberty! Independence! Could it be, man, that you have never understood it? Never wanted it? Never deserved it? Never had it? Never earned it? That you were never deprived of it by anyone except yourself?

Could it be that all the purchase price so dearly paid in the name of "liberty," the treachery of parent for child, the horror beyond all remembrance, was for a lie? For the very opposite of the promised thing?

Could it be?

Let us neither pretend to be without pretense, nor deceive ourselves about our self-deceit, nor be so stupid as to dissemble our stupidity. Time enough to evangelize ourselves when, and if, we get to heaven.

What of this book?

Will a revolutionary treatise provide an intellectual catalyst whereby the minds of millions will become transfigured and suddenly act for good government as thoroughly as they have always worked for evil? No!

Can man be apotheosized by a masterstroke of literature? No!

Do any cadavers in the mortuary of dead governments need further dissection? No!

Is there a magical word, an abracadabra, a feat of legerdemain, to be found on the dark surfaces of these still unopened pages? Are they written by another who aspires to the laureled brow, the cocked hat or the puttied shank?

Read on, angelic beast and anthropoid angel! You who, for at least forty thousand generations, have plodded after swamp lights, chased fleeting stars, sighed for sirens and sought empty Grails, read on! Who knows?

Man's soul is an enigma, buried in paradox, and hence: the Great Dilemma.

—From *The Great Dilemma*
by George Niewoehner (1963)

CHAPTER ONE

GOOD-BYE, HARD-ON

In early July, my good friend Leonard Auclair arrived at my cabin in New Hampshire to pay me a visit. When it came time for him to leave, I decided the same held true for me. I didn't pause to consider any of the consequences. I followed my instinct.

During the weeks following my rain-soaked baptism, I had started wearing clothes less and less. There was no one about, and it felt silly and unnatural to put on covering. I had nothing to hide and no one to hide it from. Certainly not Eve. What this lack of clothing did for me was insulate me from the awareness of the change in my physical appearance. There were no full-length mirrors in the cabin by which I could watch my ribs as they began to protrude or my derriere as it began to recede. And as I wasn't wearing jeans, I didn't have them to tell me I was shrinking. The surprise of that realization would be saved until the arrival of Auclair in his beat-up Volkswagen.

It was time to put on a pair of pants. At first I thought I must have somehow put on someone else's by mistake. They couldn't be the same pair I had worn into the woods! But they were. I immediately began to examine my body as if I were a member of America's weight-watching millions. Bones, I felt bones! My God, I thought, when did this happen? Where did it all go?

Leonard took one look, shook his head and smiled. A native New Englander and born philosopher, Auclair isn't given to stating the obvious. But this was too much. "Dirkee a little skinee," he said.

Knowing him as I did, I knew he wasn't speaking pidgin Chinese, but making a humorous observation of a serious situation. "Dirkee have a very heavy experience" is what he meant. I grabbed my duffle bag, my beloved cast-iron cooker, locked up the cabin with a silent thought of thanks to Michio Kushi for providing it and jumped into Leonard's flimsy excuse for a car.

On our way back to New York City, where I planned to visit Bill Dufty and Gloria Swanson before heading back to Los Angeles to tie up loose ends, we stopped in at Leonard's parents' place in the Eastern corner of New Hampshire. While there I stepped onto a bathroom scale out of curiosity to see just how much of me had been left behind forever in the New Hampshire countryside.

I weighed 152 pounds! I was shocked. I hadn't been aware of losing any weight at all and in about six weeks I had lost 23 pounds. Weight Watchers, eat your hearts out.

You may find it hard to believe that I wasn't aware of any great weight loss, but remember that the overpowering awareness of the emotional and psychological changes I was going through far overshadowed any interest in the size of my waistline. And I never was interested, never have been interested, in losing weight. I didn't go to the cabin to improve and/or change my physique. In fact, I was constantly told in the ensuing years how I had ruined the wonderful build I had while still pumping iron and gnawing bone. America loves the overdeveloped bulk of the high-protein bodybuilder. What title do we give to the huge-muscled, defined hulk who most epitomizes our ideal male body? *Mr. America*! Arnold Schwarzenegger would never, will never, covet the build of Dirk Benedict.

Besides, how can you be concerned over losing weight when you're losing something much more intrinsic to the human condition: your sex drive! Normally, spending six weeks alone in a mountain cabin will lead you to dream of the opposite sex. My own cabin retreat in Montana has given me ample room to experiment with which urges come first in the human being. After food, sex! Sex is number two with a bullet! It doesn't take many nights alone in a beautiful mountain cabin, with plenty to eat, before all of a man's sleeping and most of his waking hours are imbued with the pervading sense that something is missing: *Woman*! A guy may drive into town for all kinds of reasons . . . to get the mail, to have breakfast, dinner, lunch, to pick up some more nails, to have a beer . . . but the *real* reason is to make contact with a female. And hopefully, a female with the same thing on her mind as he has on his: the ecstatic intermingling of male/female juices of polarized energy!

Yet, it was without a whimper that my hunger for sex disappeared. I wasn't aware of its passing. For the first time in my post-pubescent life, I was waking up in the mornings without an erection! But I didn't even make note of that. Which should give you an idea of what was really going on. I always look back on 1975 and the early part of 1976, during which my Kamikaze struggle against the tumor in my prostate was at its peak, as the most profoundly aware and beautiful period of my life. This is in no small part due to the fact that I was free from the continual quest for female companionship that is part of any healthy male's adult life. I was a thirty-year-old with the body of a twelve-year-old.

Remember, the awareness of the American public has changed a great deal with regard to alternate approaches to cancer. In the seventies traditional treatment was still everyone's first choice (growing failure was yet to catch up with the American Medical Association).

So, from the moment I read William Dufty's letter on the beach in California in 1975, until the October 1983 issue of *People* magazine, I kept the entire world in the dark regarding the macrobiological history of my prostate. That circle of darkness extended to and included my own family.

Especially my own family. It is from those who know us best and love us most dearly that we have the most to fear as we struggle to follow our own road. For it is to them we are most vulnerable. Their heartfelt pleas for us to give up the madness of our ways are *very hard*, indeed, to ignore. That is, I was experiencing the state of asexuality that Adam had before he hid his manhood with a fig leaf. My sex drive left me for nearly a year. Not that I didn't enjoy the presence of female energy, but the drive to co-mingle it with my own was not there. It was a state of bliss, during which I realized the extent to which mankind's destiny has been ruled by enslavement to his genitalia.

To experience this at age thirty was quite a mind-altering adventure. I reminded myself of when I was twelve and life was an endless summer: fishing and hunting, playing baseball, playing hide-and-seek. All the so-called aimless play that only the young are capable of before male/female polarity takes over and life, more often than not, becomes a soap opera. She loves me, she loves me not. To be free from this enslavement at thirty provided me with the unimaginable serenity to focus on larger, soul-realizing issues. I could see, as the sex drive faded, how silly it all is. How exactly similar adult courting, romance and trauma are to the childhood game of hide-and-seek. It would never be the same for me.

The women I was to meet in the years after 1975, when I turned thirty going on twelve, were to find me maddeningly *free* from the influence of that magic scent they so expertly wield to control the attention of any and all men. I always accepted their forbidden fruit, but seldom accepted the strings attached. I ate the apple but declined the fig leaf!

There is a rather long list of women who could attest to my detached attitude towards them. Women who loved me or professed to love me. What they really wanted was enslavement. Mutual bondage in the name of love! Romantic realization of the sentimental motto, "We can't live without each other."

The truth is we can—any of us can—live without anybody. We can especially live without those we truly love. Love is freedom, contrary to what the behavior of most parents toward their children would lead you to believe. How tragic is their need to keep their kids forever chained, via money, guilt and a multitude of psychological chains, to the parental hearth. To never let the umbilical cord be cut, so that we end up with fifty-year-old children raising their children with the same crippling need to enslave. Living their lives through their offspring. The extent to which this is done is in direct ratio to the extent such people do *not* love their children.

Most animals in the wild not only turn their young loose when the time arrives, but furthermore, if the youngster refuses to leave, it is swatted firmly on the nose as many times as it takes for it to get the message: you're on your own!

So I refused to let the women in my life feel guilty for that initial fall from grace. It could be a game of hide-and-seek, but neither the seeker nor the sought, with her "forbidden" fruit, were to be judged by the consummation of the chase. She could run and hide while I chased and sought, but when I found and took, neither player was then committed to a relationship of responsibility. In fact, the reverse is the truth: in the synthesizing of their opposite polarities, both man and woman experience ecstatic freedom *from which* is born another *free* soul with its unique destiny to fulfill.

It wouldn't be until my return to Los Angeles and the girl-friend I had left there when I began my prostatic retreat, that I would become fully aware of the physiological fact that my sex drive was on hold. At that time, as you can well appreciate, I wondered just how long it would be like this. I knew it would return . . . or did I? I was concerned. On the other hand, life was so peaceful without the constant harrassment of needing to fornicate that it took some of the worry out of the situation.

I may not have been overly worried, but according to Impotents Anonymous, headquarterd in Chevy Chase, Maryland, an estimated ten million American men suffer from chronic impotence. They are plenty worried! If only they knew that impotence is one of the maladies most easily cured by dietary means. Its cause is not psychological, but physiological. The mental problems follow the inability to perform, which is preceded by a physiological problem created by improper and excessive eating habits. I had had periods of impotence during the last year and a half of my heavy meat-eating days. The mental anguish that followed exacerbated the problem, but first comes the physical, then the mental. Even if you don't *like* sex, it's still not mental, but physiological and curable with dietary changes.

One of the first changes I noticed when I gave up animal food in 1971 was the change in my sex drive, quantitatively and qualitatively. The impotence I experienced beginning with my New Hampshire period was for very different reasons from those in 1968–69, when I was still saturated with animal protein. The same symptom, totally antithetical causes. The first time around I was on a path of degeneration; this second bout with impotence was the result of a body busy regenerating itself.

As my body began the process of healing itself of all my past excesses, as reflected most dramatically by my prostatic tumor, it channeled all its forces to deal with the bodily functions most essential for recovery and rejuvenation. As strong as the sex drive is, you *can* live without sex. You can *not* live with aberrant cell growth in your prostate. It will, in time, kill you. The excess animal fat, protein and salt that had accumulated had been stored in various areas throughout my body. As the body started to clean house, all energy and vitality went into this process of healing through discharge.

The ability to procreate is a function of an excess of energy. My body, given what it was going through, had no excess to spare, and my ability to procreate went into hibernation.

So, when you consider the complete transformation I was going through, it's easy to understand how getting thinner slipped my attention. There were days in New Hampshire when I felt weak beyond belief. I couldn't climb the stairs to the upstairs room where I was sleeping, so I slept on the floor of the living room. This would be followed by tremendous bursts of energy: I would be up for eighteen hours and sleep for only four or five before arising again, ready to take a hike down the road on a dandelion hunt.

And I had dreams. Mostly of food. Night after night I had a recurring dream in which two hamburgers would come and talk to me. They would tell me how much they missed me. Ask what was wrong with me. Finally they would plead for me to take a bite of them. I never responded to them in my dream, but simply sat and watched as they went through their routine: sometimes talking among themselves, sometimes getting angry and threatening when I would have nothing to do with them. My later experiences with people who would try to force me to just try a piece of steak or hot dog or hamburger would be a word-for-word replay of my New Hampshire hamburger nightmares. Offering, pleading and finally trying to coerce me into validating their own dietary choice by joining in.

The cowboy in me became Kamikaze as I stuck to the task of restructuring my body and my life while enduring countless attacks over the years by those who saw my ''off-beat'' way of eating as an attack on their own dietary habits. Time and again I was told that my quack diet was going to kill me, that there was nothing wrong with meat or sugar and it wouldn't be long before I would see the error of my ways.

No matter how many times this happened—and it occurred virtually every time I was trapped in a social gathering where there was food being served and someone noticed

I wasn't eating my share of hamburgers or guzzling any Coca Cola—I was always astonished by the ferocity of the attack. I constantly wondered, and sometimes asked, why it mattered to them what I ate? I have yet to get an answer, other than the fact that they are concerned for my welfare. Can you begin to understand what goes through my mind when an overweight, balding individual with blood-shot eyes, five to ten years my junior, starts to lecture me on the evils of my choice in food?

It gets more and more difficult for anyone to tell me, as I get older and feel younger, that what I'm eating is going to ruin my health! And yet it happens. Why? I'll let you figure it out. Why do any of us take issue with another person's life when it in no way impinges on our own? Jealousy? Envy? Resentment? Or an intuitive sense of the *truth*, something we all find irritating and irresistible at the same time. Why does the heavy boozer resent the fellow who says no to the offered martini? If misery loves company, perhaps it also holds true for hardening of the arteries, arteriosclerosis or diabetes.

So, when I stepped into the suicide seat of my good friend Leonard Auclair's beat-up Volkswagen, I began a two-year odyssey "on the road." Criss-crossing America time and again on a journey, the nature of which gives validity to the title of this book. To have stayed in one place, where the quality of food (which was to decide the outcome of my treatment) could be controlled, would have been wiser, safer and the means to a speedier recovery, but the Kamikaze warrior is not concerned with safety. Death is of no concern. His journey reflects only his own instincts for accomplishing his objective. My instinct was to move. And so I almost never stopped.

CHAPTER TWO

ON THE ROAD

Leonard dropped me in the Big Apple, where I made a bee-line for the Swanson kitchen where this all began, knowing there would be warmth, understanding and *food*.

My meatless, sugarless mom opened the door, took half a step back and said, "Yes?"

Dear God, she doesn't recognize me! I thought. "It's me, Dirk, the brown-rice butterfly-boy!"

She squealed with recognition and told me later she wondered who the eighteen-year-old girl was pounding on her door.

Eighteen years old? A girl? I knew I was thin, hadn't had a haircut in months, and that the light in her doorway was of the flattering kind, but still . . . I should have known. If the keenly observant, bluer-than-blue eyes of Gloria Swanson failed to recognize me, what a nightmare of mistaken identities must lie ahead as I kept on moving along my Kamikaze Cowboy course.

My next stop was Los Angeles. My friend Richmond Johnson met me at LAX. If I hadn't seen him in the crowd, he'd still be looking for me.

"Are you all right?" he asked worriedly. "Cuz you sure as hell don't *look* all right. Maybe you should see a doctor. Just to be safe."

"No, Dick, everything's fine," I assured him. "I know I may look a little emaciated, but trust me, I know what I'm doing."

I threw my luggage—a duffel bag and one beautiful well-used, cast-iron cooking pot—into the back of his pickup and we headed for our shared digs in Manhattan Beach, just down the road a piece from L.A.

We were giving up the pad on the beach: me, because it was no longer within my financial means, and Dick, to move in with his girlfriend. But Dick had a proposition for me. Would I drive his pickup, a brand-new four-wheel-drive Chevy, to his summer home in New Hampshire? New Hampshire? Wasn't I just there?

Enroute, he would meet me in his home town, Madison, Wisconsin, where we would load the pickup with antique furniture from his parents' home and take it with us eastward. He didn't have the time or inclination to drive the entire trip himself and, knowing my rootless situation, thought I might be interested. I was. Perfect. Movement. On the road again.

I asked if it would be all right for me to take a swing through Montana on my way to Wisconsin. "Absolutely . . . just meet me there by the end of August."

My experience of mistaken identity with my adopted mom in New York should have prepared me for what was to come when I drove into White Sulphur Springs, Montana, eager to see my real mother. It hadn't! That I could have imagined my mother and sister's reaction to seeing me being any different from what it was is a testament to my own manic absorption in the larger issues with which I wrestled. I was simply oblivious to the immensely dramatic change in my entire persona and what it must have looked like to those who had known the *old* me. And no one knew the old me better than my mother.

Adding further to the shock for my mother and sister was the fact that they had no idea that I had cancer of the prostate. The number of people who *did* know I could count on one hand: Dufty, Kushi, Swanson and a couple of medical doctors. To everyone else who would come into contact with me, it was anybody's wild guess just what the hell had caused this dramatic change. The reasons for my secrecy were too numerous to list and perhaps can only be understood by someone who elects, as I did, to take the leap into the void of single, solitary self-treatment.

Perhaps by sharing a little story that happened recently on *The A-Team* set, I can give you a hint of the impossibly complex situation that could have arisen had I told those near and dear to me the real reason for my radical lifestyle. I was called from the middle of filming by one of the assistant directors to take an emergency call from the producers of the show. They informed me that I must call the doctor who had given me my preshooting physical immediately . . . there was a "problem." I called the doctor. He was in a state of shock. The insurance company who handles *The A-Team* policy had called him, questioning the results of his report on yours truly. I had passed with flying colors!

This doctor and I were, after scores of examinations, not only for *The A-Team* but numerous other productions, old friends. He marveled at the glowing statistics of my medical checkups. So he was horrified to be told by the insurance company's representative that they had heard I had *cancer* and was therefore, naturally, uninsurable.

For a second I couldn't figure out what in damnation they could be talking about; then it dawned on me: I had recently come out of the carcinogenic closet in *People* magazine, and some insurance company secretary, catching up with the latest scoop on her favorite celebrities, must have seen my confession with regard to my prostate. I told the doctor to have them reread the article and they would find that this was all very *old* news, *eight* years old, to be exact. And they would also find that I had just submitted to a complete battery of blood tests as final proof of my recovery, just in case of exactly such an occurence as this.

With all of America dropping like flies from cancer of one kind or another (and celebrities no exception), I don't blame the insurance company for their anxiety. They have computer readouts that tell them to the dime how much treatment of prostate cancer costs at Sloan-Kettering. And it ain't cheap.

So the emergency went up in the smoke of eight years of health and the results of my bloodletting, but you can imagine the nightmare that would have occurred had it been only *five* years and I hadn't had the AMA's seal of approval.

The blood that ties mother to son is very thick indeed, for it is she who has fed us in her womb, at her breast and at her table. Now I had switched from the accustomed venison, elk and beef to rice, barley and wheat. The change was *total*. Mother Nature and Father Time had become my new parents. It would take the displaced original parent, with a true mother's instincts, to realize what was going on.

"You have cancer, don't you?"

I'd forgotten my mother had worked in the local hospital for fifteen years and had seen her share of cancer victims. The yellow pallor of my skin and my general state of emaciation looked all too familiar to her. In my heart I knew I couldn't expect her to understand, so I did what I had to do. I lied.

"No, I don't. I'm just determined to find a way of eating that's free of animal foods. I'm being careful . . . and if I find it impossible, well, then I'll know. But I have to find out."

My mother hadn't spent over twenty years married to my father for nothing. She recognized an immovable mind set when she heard one. But it didn't ease the pain. Or calm the fears. That would take years.

When the time came for me to head on down the road to my rendezvous with Dick, my mom and sister watched, sobbing in the back yard, as their son and brother drove down the little back alley for what I'm sure they thought was the last time. It is those we love most to whom we must be most cruel if we are to survive.

The three-day drive from Montana to Madison, Wisconsin, took a lifetime. I sensed I was reaching a point of no return and for the first time began to wonder about the course I had chosen. I usually ate breakfast at a truck stop, which is the only place where you stand a carnivorous ghost of a chance of finding oatmeal. Not instant, sugar-coated stuff, but old-fashioned, forty-five-minutes-on-the-stove *oatmeal*. To this day, I get a warm glow and sigh a sigh of thanks whenever I see a Union 76 truckstop. It did bother me, however, that they had a "trucker's only" section, and I had to eat with those of the less heavy metal. I felt a strange kindred with the solitary life of those truckers.

Dinner was usually cooked over an open fire in some spot out of view of traffic. It consisted of rice or barley and the onions, carrots or corn that I had been lifting from the fields and gardens I drove past. I slept in the back of the pickup on hay from a couple of bales I'd stolen in a field just east of Lavina, Montana. After all the thousands of bales I'd stacked, growing up in Montana, I felt somehow that these were owed me. All this thievery of agroproducts came natural to me. I never gave it any thought. As if all things grown in the earth belonged to everyone living on the earth. More to the point, I was "on the road," stretching pennies, camping out, eating out . . . who had time to search for a grocery store?

I was on the road, and bits and pieces of Kerouac's novels began to drift through my mind as the Kamikaze quality of my journey began to make itself absolutely evident. Kerouac's Kamikaze rush toward an enlightenment he never realized was an exercise in excess. Mine was a Far Eastern example of temperance. I'd read enough of Jack to recognize a similar state of mind. I knew what had happened to him.

I arrived in Madison in the nick of time. Richmond was already there and preparing to give away his daughter's hand in marriage. After New Hampshire, Montana and the past three days on the road with Mr. Kerouac, I wasn't sure I could handle the company of hundreds of wedding guests gaily rejoicing in the beginning of another " 'til-death-do-us-part'' couple. I was strung out on rice, carrots and oatmeal. With "nothing" on the side. Strong cravings for beer, salads, fruit—all bad news for my prostate—began to overpower me.

Richmond took me to my room in the mansion that had been in his family for several generations. Its comfort was almost more than I could stand. He left me alone to prepare myself for a later entrance into the matrimonial festivities. I immediately filled the tub with hot water (a tub big enough to provide Mark Spitz room to work out) and took off my clothes. As in any home of the affluent, the room was filled with full-length mirrors. It also possessed an old-style bathroom scale, the kind you now only find in a doctor's office (or starlet's dressing room). A mirror and a scale . . . all I needed to see how my physical appearance compared to the tinge of fear growing in my mind. They compared beautifully!

I positioned all the mirrors so I could see myself in 360 degrees of diagnostic splendor. I was a sight to behold! Bones and skin and the vaguest notion of muscle. I assumed it was muscle, as it was where muscles are usually found on the human anatomy. All that was missing was the tell-tale number tattooed on my wrist.

What held my attention most as I posed and gyrated in the middle of my multireflected self, was my *ass*. I couldn't take my eyes off my ass. Throughout my life I had always been known for possessing what can only be described as a well-muscled, slightly overproportioned rear end. My friends had always attributed much of my athletic prowess to the development, size and strength of this part of my anatomy. But with my New Hampshire shrinkage, I was blatantly aware of the change in this part of me. Little did I know then that there were still more changes to come. Many more.

However, in this case there was no more to go . . . it was *gone!*

As I gazed at myself in shock and not a little horror, I wondered what kept me standing. Determination and the will to survive, I assumed. With dread anticipation I stepped on the scale. I put the big weight on 100 and the little weight on . . . Let me see: well, I weighed 152 coming out of New Hampshire, I told myself. Surely I can't weigh much less than that, no matter what the size, or lack thereof, of my derrière. So I'll put the little weight on 50 and go from there. The pointer didn't budge. Well, okay, sure, I thought, I gotta be lighter than that! After all, muscle is heavier than fat. I lost all the fat I had in New Hampshire and God knows I ain't got any muscle (at least I can't *see* any muscle) . . . so, I'll put the little weight on 45 and start adjusting down. 45 . . . 44 . . . 43 . . . Jesus, better speed this up and get it over with . . . 40 . . . 39 and still counting . . . 38 . . . 37 . . . 36 . . . I can't believe this! 35 . . . 34 . . . 33 . . . 32 . . . *Thirty-two!* I weighed 132 pounds!

When I was a senior in high school I weighed 175 pounds, 145 pounds as a freshman! When did I last weigh 132 pounds? The words of Bill Dufty came back to me: "You will go back to zero!" I had thought he meant figuratively, in some spiritual sense of the word, not literally, physically.

My little bedroom self-study had confirmed it: I had indeed reached the point of no return. I was stranded on an island between what I had been and what I dreamed of being. Would I continue to shrink (what was there left of me to melt? Bones?), or would I turn around and begin the inexorable voyage back? My mind raced as it considered the possible scenarios . . . while my physiological status remained in limbo.

Throughout this period of my life, those people who told me that I was "killing myself" were entirely correct, but not in the way they intended. I *was* killing myself. My *old* self.

My body was "dying" for the food it had been used to since the womb and not receiving it, my body was simply dying. And this included the tumor in my prostate, which was no longer receiving the "food" it needed to continue expanding. With time it began to shrink.

I simply let Mother Nature do what man tries to do with chemotherapy and radiation. They bombard the "bad" cells with chemicals and/or radiation, hoping to kill more "bad" cells than "good" cells. But the power of their machines is paltry compared to the awesome energy of the universe. And the wisdom and understanding of the medical mind is miniscule compared to the absolutely perfect understanding of Mother Nature.

Eating food that doesn't create excess for the body to deal with unleashes the omnipotent power of Mother Nature within the human body and balance is slowly restored. It is as impossible for cancerous cell growth to exist in a human being eating in accord with the universal laws by which all of nature functions as it is for orange trees to grow in Montana. Like an orange tree planted in a cold country, my old body was dying a slow but sure death at the hands of Mother Nature as every day I ate food that accorded with the infinite wisdom of the order of the universe instead of violating its precepts.

Disease and sickness are as much a reflection of Mother Nature creating balance as are health and harmony. It is only a matter of direction. If we consume more than the body needs, that excess is stored. When there is no longer any room for storing our excesses, we get aberrant cell growth, as Mother Nature attempts to maintain balance and keep the organism as a whole alive. Tumors are stored excess. Benign today, malignant tomorrow.

Reversing this process of accumulation is simply a change in direction, the melting away of excess (fat, salt, protein, mucus, oil, etc.) as the body maintains its balance. When starvation is the situation the body finds itself in, it begins eating stored fat, muscle tissue and eventually bone . . . all to maintain balance and life. I had had a lifetime of too much; it was time for not enough.

Leaving Wisconsin, I found myself in Island Pond, New Hampshire, where Richmond's family owned a beautiful summer lodge. My weight was still within pounds of that prepubescent 132. Emotionally, I was hanging on. My mental state ran the gamut from foggy bouts of nostalgia that created a melancholy beyond belief, to a state of razor-sharp psychic perception during which I saw *through* people and *nothing* missed my attention. During this entire phase, when my brain was the largest muscle of my being, I would have these periods of incredible awareness. Almost as if drug-induced. *Everything* became clear to me. I knew what people were thinking, what they were feeling, what particular nuances filled the pauses in their speech.

And I talked! Nothing could stop me. I talked about anything and everything and with a clarity that would stop people in their tracks. Four months of fasting may or may not have been having an affect on my prostate, but my brain was having the time of its life.

I was being drawn toward Boston and a visit with Kushi. It had been four months since my first visit to Michio and the beginning of my strict no-nonsense regime. His last words to me echoed in my dreams: "*Good behavior.*" He had known that would be the most difficult aspect of the journey, resisting the limitless temptations that America has to offer throughout this sugar-coated land.

In Kushi's cabin it had been easy. There were no temptations. On the road it was a different story. A constant reminder of how far "out there" I really was. More significantly, it was a constant struggle to find anything I *could* eat. Unless, of course, I had brought it with me in my knapsack from whatever brown-rice oasis I had just departed. There were only three items I found in supermarkets across the land that I could or would eat: Wheatena, oatmeal and sometimes Cornnuts, with the salt dusted off. *Everything* else was adulterated, sophisticated and polluted to one degree or another! Market vegetable sections I used as a source of last resort, due to the amount of chemicals used in growing, shipping and displaying them.

"Good behavior." Well, I knew I deserved an A+ in that department. How good my behavior would have been had it not been a matter of life and death I'll never know. The urge to pay Kushi a visit became overpowering. And what the hell . . . I was in the neighborhood.

You will never experience or understand true hospitality until you've been the guest in a traditional Japanese home. I arrived around 7:00 P.M. in the evening. It was a very cold, rainy day. I removed my shoes in the entryway and left them amid the scores of others left there by those who had come before me.

This custom of removing your footwear before entering a home has many benefits: first, it makes for a much quieter environment, without all kinds of footgear clanging around; second, it makes for a much cleaner home, as you leave the dirt of the outside world where it belongs . . . outside; third, it puts everybody at their *real* height and does away with all this three-inch heel intimidation; fourth, it provides a sensuality in walking about that the hard soles of a shoe deny you; fifth, it lets your feet *breathe*; sixth, it gives you a chance to show off your socks . . . a part of our dresswear that seldom gets seen otherwise; seventh, you can tell who is already in the house by giving the shoes outside a quick once-over, thereby avoiding contact with a person(s) you may want to avoid. I could continue, but I think you get the point.

As I entered the large hallway, I could see that dinner had just been completed. The Kushi home is a very large old Bostonian house made of stone, with a central staircase that provides access to the many rooms on each of its three stories. It is the nerve center for the macrobiotic movement throughout the United States and, indeed, the world. It serves as home, office, hospital, meeting house and halfway home for hundreds of people in the course of a day. At any given time during the twenty-four hours of any day you will find activity.

As I stood in the center of the entranceway, wondering what to do next, I could hear voices coming from all around me. Business as usual at the Kushi center. Just as I was beginning to feel maybe this wasn't the right time for me to be foisting myself into Kushi's hectic schedule, Aveline Kushi, Michio's wife, appeared, as if out of nowhere.

"Dirk, so glad to see you. Please, come, you must say hi to Michio. He will be so happy to see you."

I mentioned that I really didn't want to interrupt him, as I knew how busy he was. Aveline just smiled and pushed through the door leading into the large room where Michio was kneeling, Japanese style, in conference with four or five other people.

Michio saw me and stood immediately. He looked at me, through me and beyond. The completeness of his gaze as he took me in lasted but seconds. I knew I had just had the "consultation" I had come for. He smiled, almost laughed, as he shook my hand and nodded his head up and down.

I understood. To the world at large—friends, family, doctors—I was an emaciated, hollow-eyed sack of bones covered with a greenish-yellow layer of skin. To Michio I was yet another example of the healing power of whole foods, Mother Nature and "good behavior." The quality of his greeting said everything.

Aveline returned to tell me food was waiting. We went into the dining room. The most fantastic array of Japanese cuisine was laid out on the table in tantalizing splendor. I sat down, gave thanks, and for the next hour tried to make up for all those months of Union 76 oatmeal and my own crude cooking. Aveline continued to bring further treats to the table, knowing what it was I wanted and needed before I did.

"Please, now you must take a bath and relax."

She showed me upstairs to the bathroom. She had already run a tub of hot water. I took off my clothes and sank into the delicious warmth, wondering whether I would ever be able to climb back out. When eventually I did and stepped into the outside area to get dressed, I found my clothes gone and an all-cotton robe in their place.

Aveline arrived to show me to the room where I would be sleeping. A Japanese futon had been laid out with a beautiful down comforter for warmth. I thanked her profusely as she withdrew and I slid between the soft cotton sheets and fell instantly asleep.

The next morning I awoke to find my clothes, all freshly laundered, stacked neatly beside my head. As I lay there giving thanks for all the kindness I had been shown since arriving the night before, one of Aveline's assistants came in quietly and gave me a cup of hot bancha tea.

"How do you feel?" she inquired.

"Wonderful."

She left, telling me breakfast was available whenever I was ready. I did feel wonderful, and I felt something else, too. I felt I had turned the corner . . . I had just passed the point of no return. I was on my way back.

CHAPTER THREE

GOD BLESS CHARLIE'S ANGELS

My slide back into Hollywood went unnoticed. How else? I knew it wouldn't be easy putting the pieces of my career back together. Or fast. There's no news quite as old as the news that an actor who did a TV series and three movies, followed by two and a half years of unemployment, wants to make a comeback. Hollywood is full of them—actors who had some success, then fell on hard times. I was no exception. I'd "had my shot," my chance at success in Tinseltown. As far as casting directors were concerned, I obviously didn't have what it takes. Add to this the dramatic change in my physical appearance: a mere shadow of my former all-beef self, a self that the casting gurus *now* claimed to prefer to the new, slimmed-down, Byronesque version. It was gonna be a long road to hoe.

I didn't care, because I didn't care whether they hired me or not. I was going to keep showing up in their outer offices until I had served my time back in Hollywood and that little voice within told me it was time to move on. Whatever modicum of success came my way in the process was beside the point. I had some dues to pay. "Never do anything for money." Well, my dad didn't have to worry: Hollywood would make sure of that.

Six months of rejection finally paid off with an invitation to the party. Farrah, Jackie and Kate . . . here I come! My first gig was to be "third lead" in a segment of *Charlie's Angels*. "Third lead" in the Hollywood vernacular is a euphemism for one step above an "extra," which is a euphemism for providing "atmosphere." Which means you're one notch above being a piece of furniture. I was to be a piece of furniture with dialogue.

Aaron Spelling (producer of *Chopper One*, the series that ended my career first time around) was the producer; Kate Jackson (who had broken my heart a few years before) was one of the stars; and George Brown (who had wanted someone else for the part) was directing. It was good to be back among friends.

It wasn't a tough show to do and I had done my homework. Remember, I was an actor who had once played Ajax in *Troillus and Cressida*, for Christ's sake. Who'd played a lead on Broadway. Who'd understudied Edmund in hopes of going on opposite Charlton Heston's James Tyrone in *Long Day's Journey into Night*. Who'd done Shaw, Ibsen, Pinero, Goldoni, Sheridan, Miller, Williams. Never mind the rust of two and a half years of unemployment. I knew my lines. I was prepared.

It needn't have mattered. I could've memorized Hamlet while waiting . . . not the part, the *play!* Patience was definitely the prerequisite for this job . . . waiting, the name of the game. The name of the game played by the three stars was an entirely different kettle of fish. Suffice it to say that it was the primary concern and source of employment for more than several people on the payroll to try to get all three "stars" on the same set at the same time. This goal, once achieved, was only the beginning.

I remember mirrors. Huge, hand-held, custom-made mirrors, roughly the size of tennis rackets and wielded with the expertise of Chris Evert Lloyd by ladies who followed their designated stars around, ever on the lookout for that star's need to be reflected unto herself. I was amazed at the instinct these "holders of the mirror" had for knowing when to whip a forehand or backhand or a slicing, behind-the-back dropshot, flicking the star's image immediately into the best position for total self-study. In between scenes, in between takes, in between sentences, in between spaces of time so small there was no "in between" to get in between . . . these mirrors would be called into position, blinding the beholder with the perfection of what she saw. Not a hair, not a line of mascara, not an eyelash, not a wrinkle on a collar was ever allowed to exist in a state of disarray.

I sat and waited, blinded by the beauty of it all, wondering whether the California sun reflecting off those perpetually moving mirrors was flashing some intergalactic Morse code to the heavens above, and if so, what was the message?

For me, the message was very clear. I was *definitely* back in Hollywood.

CHAPTER FOUR

DON'T MESS WITH STARBUCK

"Now what's the problem?"

"They say he's not sexy."

"They say *what*?"

"ABC doesn't think he's sexy enough."

"That's it! I've had it! This is war!"

In the fall of 1977, nine months after I had embarked upon my re-entry into the business of make-believe for money, I was bunking with Bill Dufty and Gloria Swanson during a brief visit to New York. I had come there from Hollywood to touch bases with some of the high mucky-mucks of casting, thereby letting them know I was back again. Most of them didn't know I had left. Ah, well! My agent and personal manager at the time thought it important that I return to the city of my earlier success and "make the rounds." I agreed to it, quietly considering the list of old friends I could contact to ensure more of the exciting times New York has always seemed to hold for me.

From the palatial Fifth-Avenue digs of Swanson/Dufty, where I was living way over my economic head but in perfect spiritual harmony, it was a short invigorating stroll down the avenue to the Sherry Netherland Hotel for a "general meeting" with Glen Larson. Back in 1977 Larson was in the middle of preparing a megabuck blockbuster sci-fi project for Universal and ABC Television. Nothing like it had ever been done before on television.

Oblivious to this, or any other specific point to the meeting, I thought I was merely going to spend a few minutes making the acquaintance of one of the more successful men in television. Glen Larson was (and is) one of the most successful and prolific producers in television. He's produced such hits as *Fall Guy, Night Rider, Magnum, P.I., Hardy Boys* and *B.J. and the Bears.* A guy could do worse than hitch his wagon to such success.

Meetings were nothing new to me and I knew from past experience that they almost always amounted to nothing. They usually served the purpose of paying off old debts to various agents, etc., for past favors, such as when an agent talks one of his "star" clients into working for a producer against all that "star's" wishes. I assumed that to be the case in this instance. Some deal had gone down somewhere. God knew, no one was holding their influential breath to meet with Dirk Benedict in 1977. God knew and I knew.

"Hello, this is Dirk Benedict."

"Who?"

"Dirk Benedict."

"Just a minute, please." I held my breath.

The female voice at the other end, in the penthouse suite I had been told to call promptly at 9:00 A.M., covered the receiver with her hand. I heard a mixed, muffled dialogue with other voices in the room. I didn't have to hear the words, I knew what was going on. I was a forgotten appointment no one wanted to remember. I had unwittingly become their wake-up service.

Great, I thought to myself. The perfect atmosphere in which to make an entrance. Expecting to be put off until another "more appropriate" (later?) date, I was astonished to hear the woman on the end of the line ask me to give them fifteen minutes and then "come on up!"

Jesus, I thought, they think I said Dirk *Bogarde*!

The penthouse I made my hesitant entrance into sixteen minutes later contained Glen Larson, Charles Engels, a vice-president in television at Universal Studios, and Mrs. Engels.

They had been up late. Sleep was in their eyes, or was it massive disinterest? I was thinking of who I would call to have breakfast with at nine-thirty, as I exited the Sherry Netherland.

An hour later I hit Fifth Avenue still laughing. If Glen Larson, Charlie Engels and Dirk Benedict had had their astrological charts done, perhaps it wouldn't have been a surprise to anyone. As it was, I think they were as surprised as I was over the event. It was fun! Like old friends, we never did discuss business, but rather spent the time laughing and kidding each other. Having an experience instead of talking about separate ones that the others hadn't shared.

Out of this brief hour of biochemical history was born the character "Starbuck." Written out of the facile, fertile mind of Glen Larson to be played by me in his fourteen-million-dollar, three-hour epic for ABC Television called *Battlestar Galactica*.

The script arrived at my doorstep (literally) in December. I flipped. It was the kind of light, comedic, romantic lead I had always loved playing. I had a job! I was to be paid for doing what I would do for nothing. More importantly, I could complete the cycle I realized back in the woods of New Hampshire in 1975 *must* be completed before I could continue my Kamikaze journey. Before I could come in from my walk in the New Hampshire rain.

But there was one hitch. ABC Television Network said *no*. No, we do not see Dirk Benedict in that part (never mind that it was created for me), nor do we intend to cast him in that part. Find somebody else.

As far as Universal and Glen Larson were concerned, *I* was their choice. To assuage the network, they agreed to test a number of actors selected by casting departments at both ABC and Universal. This group of hopeful actors included Dirk Benedict.

Thus began a series of screen tests which, if strung

together, could fill an entire hour of commercial television. After a series of three screen tests in which at least ten actors were tested, things remained exactly where they had been. Universal wanted me; ABC wanted someone, *anyone*, else!

Now it began to get ugly. And very, very funny, in the ludicrous way only those who are truly detached can enjoy. After failing to find an actor they preferred over me, Glen and Universal wanted to know, specifically, what the problem was with Dirk Benedict. Why *wasn't* he right for the character of Starbuck, mischievous con man and intergalactic womanizer? they asked ABC.

"He's too lightweight," ABC replied. "Not serious enough to handle the more dramatic aspects of the teleplay."

"No problem," Glen told me after relaying this information. "We'll just do another screen test where you cry your eyes out and don't crack one itsy-bitsy, teensy-weensy joke. We'll show them *serious*."

Crank up the cameras, turn on the lights, action! Cut to:

"He isn't strong enough to handle the 'tough-guy' image so necessary for the part in dealing with outerspace bad guys."

"Simple," said Glen. "We'll just do another screen test where you beat the shit out of every kind of avionic, cyclonic, outsized, monsterish threat to the forces of good and righteousness that my typewriter can come up with!" Lights, camera, action! Cut to:

"We're not sure he can handle the love scenes. He's a bit young to be playing opposite most of the leading ladies working in television today."

Glen seemed unphased by it all. I admired his tenacity.

"But Glen, I'm thirty-two goddamn years old!" I told him. "Who are they gonna get to play opposite me, Helen Hayes?"

"Don't worry, kid," said Glen, "I'll write a love scene that'll make you look like the next Cary Grant. And I know just the girl to play opposite you."

Sure hope it isn't Katharine Hepburn, I thought to myself. Things were getting crazy.

Never mind . . . lights, camera, action! Cut to:

"He's just not sexy enough!"

This record-breaking set of screen tests began in early January of 1978 and continued until February 25. The production went before the cameras on March 3. Lorne Greene was playing the leader, "Adama," and Richard Hatch had been cast as "Apollo," Starbuck's cohort. Starbuck himself remained in limbo.

Every card had been played. It had gone from the ridiculous to the sublime. Only not everyone was laughing.

ABC knew that if they delayed long enough, it would get very costly to shoot around the character, while everyone bickered over which actor should play him. At which point the network was betting Universal would acquiesce so they could slide in the actor of *their* choice, who had been waiting patiently all the while as the screen-test marathon ran its course. Nine times out of ten—999 times out of 1,000—this works perfectly, as I would find out five years later, with NBC and *The A-Team*, when once again a network would refuse to hire me for a role created for me. This time it was the character "Face," and I was hired only after they had filmed the premier episode of the series.

But back in 1978, for the first time in anyone's memory, a network, for all its monolithic power, would *not* get its way. Frank Price was head of all television production at Universal Studios. He wanted to know why one of the main characters had yet to be cast *three days* after principal photography had begun! *And* after the studio had gone to the trouble and expense of catering to every one of the network's whims in their demand for screen test after screen test, looking for an actor whom everyone at Universal (producer, writer, director, casting department) agreed had already been found!

"*Now* what's the problem?" asked Frank Price.

"They say he's not sexy," replied the distraught head of casting.

"They say *what*?"

"ABC doesn't think he's sexy enough."

"That's it! I've had it! This is war!"

The war was fought in a Bel Air residence over the weekend of March 6 and 7. I have only heard rumors of what took place. Rumors too wild to be true. I'll never know for sure what happened, but I do know that on March 8, 1978, I went to work playing Starbuck in *Battlestar Galactica*.

During my New Hampshire walk in the rain and the revelation that I must return to show business, I knew it wouldn't be easy. What I *didn't* know was that it would be *insane*!

CHAPTER FIVE

TO HAVE AND HAVE NOT

When I returned to my "career" in late 1976, it was after two and a half years of unemployment as an actor, most of which were spent totally focused on the area of my prostate and the intense scrutiny of the later spiritual ramifications and manifestations. Out of the rain of New Hampshire and into the frying pan of Hollywood.

But this time I was ready. I'd hired the prerequisite agent, of course, but I had also put a personal manager on the payroll. When *Battlestar Galactica* materialized, I further increased the size of my entourage by hiring one of the best publicists in the business, a very well-recommended business manager and a top-notch lawyer specializing in entertainment, whose client list included Sylvester Stallone. Dirk Benedict was finally in show business. Bring on the close-ups!

On the surface, and to all those involved with my career, the situation was self-evident. I was a young actor with a modicum of charm, looks, poise and personality. A "commodity." I was, thanks to *Battlestar Galactica*, about to be seen by millions of people every week in a television program that was being ballyhooed across the country as the biggest, hottest, spaciest show ever seen on earth. The character I was portraying was young, sexy, mischievous, with just the right amount of con-man anti-heroic charm to make him macho and vulnerable at the same time.

The marketing potential was enormous and to all concerned, self-evident. Here was an actor, entity, commodity with a very real shot at the brass ring. That same brass ring that Tom Selleck would so deftly grab via *Magnum, P.I.* only two short years after *Battlestar Galactica* unraveled and all those involved scrambled to salvage what momentum they could from the vacuum left by its demise.

But in the summer of 1978 we were busy filming what everyone *knew* would be *Star Wars, Bonanza* and *Little House on the Prairie* all rolled up into one gigantic festival of special-effects wizardry. Lorne Greene, Richard Hatch and myself were on the covers of *Time, Newsweek, TV Guide* and *People* magazine, to say nothing of the hundreds of lesser publications that were oh, so eager to have us gracing their covers in all our intergalactic splendor. We reeked of success.

Success in the air is like blood in the water to the sharks that inhabit the murky depths of Hollywood. Unless you have been there, it is impossible to describe. To be a celebrity in a country that worships at the altar of television, that idolizes with religious fervor the faces that glow in the dark of their living rooms, is to be the closest thing to royalty that this democratic nation has to offer. It's no small wonder that being a celebrity is addictive beyond description, dreamed of by an entire country and sought after by millions.

And there I was in September of 1978, about to lose my nearly virginal anonymity in the three-hour blitzkrieg of *Battlestar Galactica*'s premiere. The summer-long media blitz had had its predictable effect. The ratings were socko. ABC was euphoric, Universal was euphoric. Glen Larson was euphoric. My agent, my manager, my money man were all euphoric. Even my mother was euphoric: at last her son was making something of himself in the real world. The "real" world of glamour, hype and glitz.

Ah, well, how could she, a lady who had spent her entire life in the real world of down-to-earth Montana, be expected to know it was only make-believe? Only a dream, an illusion? And in the case of *Battlestar Galactica*, more essentially a mirage. But on the eve of our debut the state of mind for all concerned was full-blown *euphoria*. My people knew their

Product, Dirk Benedict, of which they all had their various percentages, was about to become a hot item. The brass ring was but a few rungs away on the ladder of success as King of Television's Leading Men.

What no one knew—not my personal manager, agent, business manager, lawyer, publicist, not even my dear down-to-earth-Montana-born-and-bred mom—what no one knew, save me and the wild strawberries in a patch of never-forgotten woods, was that I *didn't care*. Euphoria or disenchantment, success or failure, brass ring or booby prize . . . it all amounted to the same thing when seen through the eyes of a Kamikaze Cowboy. Opposite sides of the same Hollywood coin. What mattered was that I finish my journey through Celluloid City, complete with the spiritual hazard of tapping into America's consciousness via ratings success and the resultant celebrity status.

With *Battlestar Galactica* came "overnight success"! I'd been supporting myself for eight years solely from whatever sums of money I made as an actor, appearing in numerous repertory theatres across America, starring on Broadway, in films and on television. But now I was an "overnight" success. While this turn of speech may be inaccurate in terms of time, it is completely accurate with regard to exposure. Overnight I went from not even being in the kitchen, smack-dab right into the microwave! Things were heating up! There wasn't a nook or cranny of my life that didn't escape the media's manic need for manufacturing celebrities. Yes, indeed, a *star*, albeit of television, was about to be born.

How could I begin to tell all those working on behalf of my apparent goal of being a TV star that I was off the hook? Free from the addiction of having to have? Not concerned with the *result*, but only with the *process*? It was an impossible conversation to have. We can only communicate at a level of awareness common to all parties concerned. My "reality" was different from theirs. A reality altered beyond measure by the carcinogenic-induced odyssey that changed my *dream*. Freedom was mine. The ability to have and to have not was mine to do with as I saw fit. It was impossible for me to pretend to a covetousness I didn't possess.

The detachment of self from the ecstasy and agony of my career would manifest itself in a million idiosyncratic quirks. Sources of irritation and frustration, large and small, to all who dealt with me. But it had its positive side. Agent and manager didn't have to hold my hand to help me through the depression of a professional setback. There were no displays of temperament as my ego was rubbed the wrong way by a bad review, or incorrect reportage in the tabloids. I was even-tempered. Free. As free from the ego-inflating ecstasy of flattery as from the ego-depressing agony of insult. I never complained at the long hours and constant demand on my energies that is the nature of filming a television program. "So easy to get along with" was the phrase I heard time and again to describe myself. It made me a joy to work with, but impossible to predict and, more disturbing to the machinery of manufacturing stardom, impossible to control.

I could say "yes" as easily as "no" to the tinseloid tidbits that came my way as the result of *B.G.*'s resounding blast-off into the 1978–79 television season. So, mainly I said "yes." I said "yes" to the hundreds of requests for interviews in newspapers and magazines across the land. "Yes" to Merv Griffin, Mike Douglas and Dinah Shore. "Yes" to this personal appearance and that Gala Opening. "Yes" to celebrity tennis and celebrity skiing and even celebrity cooking (what's brown rice?). And "yes" to guesting on the *Donny and Marie Show*.

Here I said "yes" twice, the first time for professional reasons and the second time for more personal ones. I would have said "yes" *thrice*, but Marie had other dreams, and as the moon slowly rose over the mountains of Utah, she said "*no*." The deal was she'd give up ice cream if I gave up cigars. A new slant on incompatability.

The view from the top of the heap was a new one for me. I didn't want to miss any of the opportunities for experiencing what had heretofore been unavailable as I languished at the bottom of the heap. When this was over, as I knew it would be (everything that has a beginning has an end), no one would be able to tell me what it was like to star in a television series. I would *know*.

I criss-crossed the country, fulfilling obligations, devouring all that being a celebrity had to offer. Knowing, with each experience, that there would be no curiosity to do it again. Not in this lifetime. And *not*, as my inner voice rejoiced, in any lifetime to come. I was evolving! My gluttony knew no bounds as the huge appetite I had always had for all things devoured everything the cornucopia of show business had to offer.

What those around me mistook for ambition was, in fact, my fervent desire to eat, chew, digest and discharge *all of it*, thereby completing a cycle that had begun fifteen years earlier as I strolled innocently onto the stage of Whitman College's theatre department and sang, prophetically enough, "Only Make Believe."

For whatever reasons (no one has yet figured out what induces the American Public to turn their collective knobs to any particular channel on any given hour), *Battlestar Galactica* failed to live up to its blockbuster beginning. The ratings sagged and finally settled to a level which would have been sufficient for the continuation of any other show. But not for a project which had *numero uno* written all over it by everyone months before it went on the air. Anything but the top was too near the bottom and not good enough. In May of 1979 it was canceled, and the glory that was to be Dirk Benedict's went to Tom Selleck and others whose faces fill the spotlight illuminating the media's chosen few.

Euphoria was no longer the prevailing state of mind. Shock, dismay, astonishment, sadness, anger—all these emotions and more filled the hearts and minds of those involved with the glory that was once *Battlestar Galactica*, and more specifically, the career of Dirk Benedict. Disenchantment filled the lives of all . . . save one: I *didn't care.*

There would be other television shows in the career of Dirk Benedict, or there wouldn't. I didn't know where *Battlestar Galactica* had come from. I knew I wouldn't know where the next show was coming from. Or, indeed, if there would be a "next show." It didn't matter. As we say in Montana, I had other fish to fry.

CHAPTER SIX

ON BEING A SEX SYMBOL

Before *Battlestar Galactica*, if I wanted to meet a girl, I had to make an effort, court, woo, take a chance. This required an extension of self involving time, energy, imagination and various amounts of money. And like fishing, to which I always compared the process of searching out the perfect woman, you could never be guaranteed of "hooking" her interest once you did find her. Regardless of the amount of time, energy, imagination and money you invested . . . more often than not, you remained alone, wondering what went wrong. Not realizing it doesn't matter *what* you do; if the woman *wants* you, she'll have you, in spite of yourself. And if she doesn't, she won't.

Fortunate is the man who wakes up to this fact. And even more happy is the romancing gent who happens upon the realization that the only *real* value to the whole process of boy-meets-girl, with all its infinite plots and subplots, is not whether you live happily ever after or not, but rather that you enjoy the *chase*. As with all things, it is through the journey that you experience life, not in the achievement of the sought-after goal.

Having paid my romantic dues, I was gratefully aware of all this in 1978. What I wasn't ready for was the intervention of the ABC Television Network in my love life. As *Starbuck*'s charismatic, devil-may-care personality beamed into the living- and *bed*rooms of America, Dirk Benedict tagged along. When the film company shut down for the day or weekend, Dirk Benedict went out into the real world, while Starbuck wisely stayed behind, waiting for the beginning of another shooting day. But the public didn't seem to notice. More and more, I began to be mistaken for him.

I was no longer in control of which women I wanted to meet and/or court and/or bed. Television had become my dating service. I had a million cupids searching America for my perfect female experience. Cupids named Sony, RCA, General Electric, Quasar, Mitsubishi. All fervently shooting arrows into women across the land, casting for that woman who could bring happiness into the romantic life of Dirk Benedict/Starbuck. Thank God Glen Larson hadn't handed me a glass slipper along with the character of Starbuck.

I have yet to find a fan-mail service capable of fulfilling all the letter-writers' demands for furthering their relationships with Starbuck/Benedict. Nothing was satisfactory: if I answered their letter, I received two more with requests for an autographed picture. Send them the photo and they wanted dinner. Take them to dinner and they wanted breakfast. Then weekends together. Then, "Why didn't you call?" Then a relationship! Babies, marriage . . . everything! They wanted more than I could give to one person in one lifetime, let alone a million. They think that because they know you, you know them. (Paul Newman, Robert Redford, Tom Selleck, my heart goes out to you.)

The quantity of these women wanting to form relationships was staggering. It caught me by surprise. We all know what happens to quality as quantity increases. And of even more concern to me was the harsh reality that I was no longer in control of my love life.

Having just spent the last four years getting my prostate back into working order, I found it ironic that this should be the area of my life that would now be of such keen interest to females and the "Oral Majority" of America. And I thought *freedom* was mine!

After food . . . sex. How the batting order in the game of human desires slipped my mind, I attribute to the fact that my sex life had only been returned to me for a couple of years. I was just barely past my second bout with puberty. I may have been off the feed lot of America, off the bovine nipple of America, but I was not off the romantic treadmill of America. I had yet to let go of my emotional, psychological craving for female companionship. It was something I had to have. And I was certainly in the right place at the right time to have all thirty-two flavors.

The confusion of physical, emotional, psychological *need* with *love* is a debilitating state of mind that does for psychiatrists and lawyers what diabetes and heart disease do for doctors and surgeons. Makes them rich. Makes them rich, while it does nothing to remedy the source of all the mismatching that permeates American society today.

Contemporary America is barely hip to the "revelation" that relationships based solely on sex, no matter how fantastic, don't last. A one-night orgiastic quickie, though it may tap you into infinity for a split second or two, is not a basis by which to begin a "meaningful" relationship. Biological chemistry and spiritual harmony do not necessarily go hand in hand. An incredible blow job may blow your mind, but it will not bring you everlasting happiness. For this astounding level of awareness people pay millions of dollars to gurus of various national origins. Or worship at the altar of Dr. Ruth and other TV personalities.

If not physical attraction, then on what *does* America base the hopes and dreams of its mating masses? *Emotional* compatability, usually. Sharing the same sentimental frame of mind. Moonlit strolls, candlelight dinners, incense burning throughout love sessions of Gothic ambience.

How fleeting is the life of an emotion! Pick any of them on the spectrum, running the gamut from hate to love, and upon reflection you'll realize how fickle our emotional life of "feelings" truly is. Feeling good, feeling bad, feeling happy, feeling sad . . . the time span of any of them can usually be counted in minutes, sometimes hours, days or months.

Months . . . about the unit of time now used to measure the length of many marriages. "I just don't 'love' you anymore!" Where did it go? That wonderful "can't-live-without-you" feeling. It probably disappeared with a change in your blood-sugar level. The emotional rollercoaster on which most lives and relationships are lived is a wild and crazy reality. A yo-yo existence funded by MacDonald's, Baskin-Robbins, Wendy's, Swenson's, Kentucky Fried Chicken. Fast food, fast sex, fast love.

I have a wacky, witty, wonderful ex-pro-footballer-turned-artist friend who is much more the man of jocular ejaculation than I ever was and who maintains that "Sometimes love only takes a second." Has he learned nothing from Hugh Hefner, Warren Beatty and other playboys of the Western world who have devoted their entire lives to proving that it isn't *love* that "only takes a second," but the desperate physical and/or emotional *need* to have, to possess? A possession that lasts for whatever length of time that physical/emotional need lasts. Which could be anywhere from the time it takes to erect and eject, to the time it takes the candles to burn out, to the time it takes to realize that he/she squeezes the toothpaste from the wrong end. Or doesn't use it at all.

Physical love, *emotional* love . . . what next? The *mind*. *Psychological, intellectual, ideological* love. Couples who mate out of a psychological need do so to provide the crutches necessary to continue, thereby negating the necessity for any further psychological maturity. The girl who never let go of her daddy and who finds an older man to treat her as his "little girl," no matter what number the biological clock tells her is her age. Or the man looking for a replacement for his mamma. Relationships built on such interlocking disabilities last, with all their complicated angst and trauma, for only as long as the psychological incapacities of the involved parties remain constant.

Intellectual, ideological love: affection for a mate based on a premise of shared philosophies and worldly goals. Those who care for each other on this level of human experience are most rare, for few take the time to reflect and study and discover what their life philosophy is. A mate chosen at this level of awareness can be yours for a lifetime. Erosion of physical beauty, fluctuations in emotional states, changes in psychological needs . . . all can come and go as the relationship continues, because of a shared *dream* in the material world.

There is another dimension to our lives that can be the basis for loving a member of the opposite sex (and indeed, the world). It is so rare as to be almost nonexistent and of interest to few reading these pages, but it is my dream for the world. *Spiritual love.* A love beyond any and all physical, emotional, psychological, intellectual needs. A love born out of a shared *dream of freedom*, capable of surviving for an eternity and of changing the world.

CHAPTER SEVEN

NO MORE MR. SPERM BANK

The girl who would finish the job that Monica started back in 1971 came into my life in 1977. Joann was everything I had ever dreamed of finding in a woman (save one thing, which I was yet to dream of): five-foot-two (she always lied about her height, so why shouldn't I?), perfectly in proportion, witty, athletic, vital, perceptive, passionate, intelligent, ever-optimistic and eager for any and all adventures. She fit in completely, be it Montana rustic or Beverly Hills chic.

We fell in love. This is *it*, I thought. The effortless expression of what man and woman together should be. Monica was a distant memory. I had shed so many layers of old self in the six years since her lesson, it never entered my mind that I might still have more to learn where women were concerned.

We were in love. *Battlestar Galactica* was a huge success. I was in the brand-new, full-blown health of the "new" me. My New Hampshire dream had become Hollywood reality. Together, she and I could and would have it all.

Her husband didn't think much of the whole situation. He was an ingredient I hadn't counted on. But I knew that with time, even he would understand how perfect his wife and I were together.

Time *did* pass . . . weeks became months became years . . . two years, to be exact. I was on location in Northern California doing a little action-adventure film called *Ruckus* when the axe fell in the form of a phone ringing in my motel room. I answered, expecting to hear that Joann was coming to see me. I had asked her to come.

"Dirk, I'm not coming. Not now, not ever. It's over. You must forget about me. Please don't hang onto the dream of us together. You must let go." Yes, she did say "let go" —stole the phrase right out of my very own personal lexicon of soap-box philosophy. Faster than you can say "Bell Telephone," my mind raced back to New York and Monica's final exit from my life eight years earlier. Unable to speak the truth, I uttered the ultimate lie: "I understand."

I had understood nothing. I understood only my love for her. I was oblivious to the truth of what she felt. The falling axe of her phone call drove the final nail into the coffin in which I could at last bury the notion that I, or any of my sex, control or decide things! Women, limited only by the level of their own awareness of it, possess all the *real* power in the course of human events . . . be they matters of the heart or otherwise.

What Joann, with all that perception and intelligence I loved so dearly, understood was that we didn't share the same *dream*! She had heard and, in fact, provided me with a soap box for my philosophic meanderings on the truth of what my *real* dream was all about. She had understood the rocky road and unpredictable existence such an approach to life guarantees. She made a choice. It was not for her.

I was left holding the phone. The wound from her falling axe took years to heal, but in that period of recuperation, I finally and forever quit giving my soul's commitment to any form of human bonding save one: *spiritual*. Realizing at the same time it would be the *woman* who would discover our spiritual compatability, not me.

I was off the romantic hook. I was ready. And waiting. Whether such a female existed or not, I hadn't a clue. But the pressure cooker of romance that *Battlestar Galactica* had exposed me to, coming to a boil in the relationship with Joann, had given me plenty of statistics on which to base my lack of expectations. I sensed that the woman of my dreams lived in some foreign land, free of Western society's "liberated" mores. I began to think Japanese. American women were too busy becoming breadwinners to have any interest in becoming bread makers.

Pamela, Bambi, Lynn, Monica, Kate, Maureen, Lucy and Denise, Kelly, Erica, Luci, Joann, Valerie, Gay Anne, Suzanne, Sue . . . twenty years of loving, 1961 to 1981. This list is partial, but each name represents the climax of a period of general dating. To each of these ladies I am grateful beyond words, for each, in her own way, nudged me ever closer to the realization and fulfillment of a *dream*. The dream of a male/female union founded on spiritual harmony. A dream that each, in her own way, did not share or believe possible to attain. Through the living of each of these relationships, I was dragged kicking and screaming to the point at which I could finally "let go" of all the physical, emotional and psychological attachments I possessed for the opposite sex. I no longer cared.

The pain and joy of each experience was excruciating, and they all had a beginning, a middle and an end. For they all began and ended in the material world of human personalities. That *endless love* that every romantic writer worth his royalty fee thinks he is writing about, and which every celluloid love story pretends to portray, gives the lie to its title and ends in the final chapter, the final reel. The beginningless, endless love that is my dream of freedom must wait until I meet the female of my male, the yin of my yang, the winter of my summer, the sharer of my spiritual dream of *absolute freedom*. A woman who, like myself, has taken the time to reflect and grow, to understand and love herself more than anything else in this world. *Before* committing that self to another.

CHAPTER EIGHT

WHERE HAVE ALL THE MOTHERS GONE?

For the past twenty years, while enjoying the growing planetary promiscuity, it has been my experience that when, as a
male, you offer—indeed, insist—that a woman take charge
and accept absolute responsibility for being the one who decides, she retreats into an infinite array of helpless persona.
All victims . . . from Daddy's little girl to Kate Millet's
liberated barracuda.

God blessed woman with the ability to create the quintessential work of art . . . the human being. It is inside her that
the human organism is created. As in all acts of creation, it
is an experience that defies description. Heifitz could never
explain why, when he played the violin, it emitted a sound
so unique as to be given his name to distinguish it. Olivier
has admitted total frustration with the fact that on the nights
when his performances are their most magnetic, he doesn't
understand the how and why of it.

There is a long list of artists who know in their souls that
they cannot honestly take credit for the work of art that the
world greets with wild acclaim. A world that is only too
eager to encourage them to take the credit. "Yes, I am a
genius, the most unique, wonderful, superhuman artist in my
field!" But in the still dark of the night, staring into the abyss
that is their creative center, they *know* that the wonderful,
intelligent, poetic, tormented personality through which they
con the world has absolutely nothing to do with it. Not
really. Not anymore than this typewriter has anything to do
with a resultant declarative sentence. (Would to God I was
capable of such wonderful simplicity.)

The typewriter is a machine, and so also is the human mix of qualities that comprises any so-called artist's personality. But none of the various aspects of one's personality are responsible for his creative acts. The source goes way beyond . . . or deeper in . . . or farther out. The source is other than the sensorial world in which we hang our pictures, play our concertos, read our novels. The artist is simply the conductor *through which* the creative spark passes. How difficult it is for any artist to come to grips with this, to admit that his world-renowned creative works have nothing to do with him and, in fact, exist only because and to the degree that he was able to get his ass out of the way.

Get out of the way. A neat trick. I think the truth is that most artists stumble upon this by accident. They look at the results of their creative ''effort'' and privately wonder where in the hell it came from. And more importantly, and certainly more frighteningly, how the hell will they ever do it again? F. Scott Fitzgerald, Hemingway, Faulkner—all alcoholic artists who lived their lives in a state of anxiety and fear of being found out that it was not they who wrote, but the hand of God.

And how many books have in truth had any real effect on the world's destiny as it claims to struggle toward a Golden Age? Damn few! The Bible? The Book of *I-Ching*? The Koran? Maybe. *Portnoy's Complaint*? *The Great Gatsby*? *The Sun Also Rises*? *The Betsy*? *Scruples*? I doubt it. The world could get along very nicely without all this drivel.

The truth is, there are very few books worth reading, songs worth listening to, paintings worth gazing upon, singers worth hearing, plays worth seeing, poems worth reading, films worth viewing, dancers worth watching. They are worthless! Junk entertainment. Distractions. They are not reaffirmations of a divine universal soul, but rather the emotional, intellectual discharges of sick people inflicting their *diseases* on their fellow man.

But did you ever see, hold, touch, watch or otherwise

come in contact with a baby who wasn't worth the seeing, holding, touching, watching? It is the ultimate work of art! And guess what? Heifitz, Picasso, even Shakespeare in his genius beyond comprehension, were incapable of creating one.

How pale seem all of *man*kind's creations when compared to the creation all *woman*kind is capable of. And guess what: this *artist*—who through the innate grace of God is capable of getting herself out of the way, letting go and giving the world what no body of scientific wizards has yet come a million light-years close to understanding or recreating, the human being—is *bored*.

The contemporary joke of all this is that women, in their spiritual ignorance, want liberation, *freedom*, so they can be free to imprison themselves in the bloody, despairing, mostly profane trenches of the world's marketplace and create . . . *what*? . . . money. The creation of life they find boring. Insulting. Creative homemaking is punishment. It's like Rubinstein being angry that he doesn't get to tune the piano before each concert; or Michaelangelo being hurt because he can't dig the marble from the quarry himself.

How terrifyingly sad that womankind has turned her collective back on the creation of family. The salvation of the world depends on the quality of that blood stream. She creates world destiny. Men control the stock market, advance ticket sales to the Super Bowl, the speed limit on freeways. Men create havoc. But women have the power of procreation, connection to the continuum of the universe, the creation of world harmony, health, happiness and order. But not unless they take control of their private kingdoms up and down the streets of the neighborhoods of the world and create harmony, health and happiness in their own homes!

Men have no choice. They are stuck with their worldly dreams—to build a bridge, write a book, start a fishing business in Alaska, pave a highway. They need their dreams of these little accomplishments. It is all God has allowed them.

They are fodder for the machinery that drives the world, expendable. Unlike the female, whose health and position in the world is essential for the future of mankind.

There are two things mankind cannot evolve without: food and sex. Women control the quality of both. They cannot escape this God-given role in the universal mechanism that allows for planetary evolvement. As men, we can only pray that along with their position of biological superiority, women will also accept resonsibility.

CHAPTER NINE

SURVIVAL

On April 13, 1983, I went to the Van Nuys Airport to wash my airplane in preparation for flying home to Montana. It was early—6 A.M.—but I felt like I'd slept in, as only four days earlier we had finished filming our first season of *The A-Team*, which involved weeks on end of getting up at 5:00 A.M. The sun was even beginning to rise.

Washing an airplane is nothing like washing your car; it takes a good four hours to do a complete and credible job. I could have hired somebody to do it, as I now had a few bucks in the bank. Indeed, the airplane had just been bought with *A-Team* loot. But I believe we must always do as much of our own labor in life as is humanly possible.

Besides, I enjoyed the exercise and having the spare time in which to do something as lazy and pressure-free as scrubbing down my brand-new airplane. All manual labor can be a form of meditation, a process of centering, which leaves us with a feeling of satisfaction and fulfillment that can never come from sitting behind a desk. Or standing in front of a camera. Go out in your back yard and dig a hole six feet deep. I guarantee you will feel better for it. If that's too overwhelming, try washing the dishes, dusting, raking the yard . . . and as you do these manual tasks, put *all* of your self into them. Concentrate on getting the dish clean, the piano dust-free, the lawn free of leaves, and do the best job you're capable of. When you're finished, sit down and enjoy the fruits of your labors. It will rid you of untold anxieties, tension, restlessness.

The problem with most of increasingly corporate America's work force is they never accomplish anything! Not really. Papers turned into more papers with different colors, different totals, different return addresses. Intangible. Abstract. Busy work. Meaningless functions void of any *real* result. Go home and cook dinner. That is real.

A lifetime of shuffling papers, taking memos, signing deals, writing contracts, is a lifetime spent missing the point. No wonder all those lawyers, business executives, real-estate agents go to the gym at the end of the day and lift weights, pump iron or go jogging. For at last, if only for a few minutes of their day, they do something *real*. They *know* how many pounds they lift, how many miles they run. They are amazed at how ''good'' they feel after their little workouts. They become *addicted*. As well they should. Before there was money, before there was fame, before there were doctors, lawyers, professions of any kind . . . before man began to abstract the life experience . . . there was happiness and contentment.

Months of working on *The A-Team* had not made me happier or more contented. It had challenged my ability to remain so. The hours of waiting, talking and thinking on the set needed to be balanced by some good honest airplane scrubbing. The winter of '83 had been a cold one by California standards and the day I chose to wash my plane was one of the first hot, sunny days of the coming summer. I pulled my Turbo 182 Cessna RG into the wash area and began spraying, scrubbing, rinsing, spraying, scrubbing, rinsing . . . ridding the plane of a winter's worth of grime, grease, dust and oxidization.

Three hours into my labors and nearing the end of this joyous physical exertion, I began to feel light-headed. Perhaps it was time to get something to eat? I paused briefly to let myself center a bit. Nothing. The sensation persisted. I sat down for a couple of minutes. Still no change. Well, I'm so close to finishing, I thought, I'll just hurry up with the finishing touches and zip home for some food and a shower. That'll do the trick!

I crawled under the plane to finish wiping down the belly. Almost immediately I felt nauseous. Whoa! What was this? Rapidly I began scrubbing, hoping to get the belly wiped clean before crawling out and standing upright to get my bearings straight. I couldn't make it. The sense of impending regurgitation became overpowering. I scrambled weakly from under the plane and held onto the wing strut as I pulled myself upright. Twelve years of being my own doctor told me that this was serious. I was weak, light-headed, sick to my stomach and feeling even hotter than the exercise and hot day warranted. Sweat began to pour from me.

Suddenly I had a strangely familiar, odd sensation. As if I had to urinate, but with a slight burning sensation right at the end of my penis. The sense that I must urinate became quickly stronger, while at the same time my bladder felt empty. This burning, itching feeling in my urinary tract, and especially at the head of my penis, felt altogether too familiar. Surprise, surprise, surprise!

Before I could ask for help to return my plane to the tie-down area, the pain and the need to relieve it via urination became unbearable. I walked as quickly as my weakened and disoriented state would allow to the nearest restroom. As I stood at the urinal unzipping my pants to relieve myself of this growing mixture of pain, itching and pressure, another pilot walked into the restroom and up to the adjoining urinal.

Oh God, I thought, just what I want least . . . an audience for whatever's about to happen. For I knew, as I stood there dripping with sweat and trying my damnedest not to attract undue attention, that what was about to come out of the end of my pecker was *not* going to be your run-of-the-mill, garden-variety pee. Nosiree. I knew this was going to be special. I prayed that my pissing companion would be brief, but my heart sank as I noticed (out of the corner of my eye, mind you) that he was unbuttoning his pants. Just my luck. I stood there, continuing to drip moisture from every part of me except the one that screamed for it the most. It's like being constipated. You need to, you want to, you struggle with every muscle and brainwave to do it . . . but nothing happens!

I couldn't imagine my peeing partner in the cockpit of an airplane if it took him this long to do something as simple as unbutton his Levi's. Then of course, the inevitable: I knew he was wondering what the hell was taking *me* so long? And why was I sweating so profusely? The only thing that made this standing piss-off (or pissing stand-off) bearable was the unbearable pain growing in my penis as I tenderly held it and begged for relief. I could endure any humiliation if only I could get through what past experience told me was coming.

Suddenly there it was, that old-time feeling. Deep inside. Way down south, where those wonderful, ecstatic climaxes of ejaculation come from. And this old-time feeling begins the same way . . . from far off, but as it comes nearer, its message becomes clear . . . this is *not* the old-time feeling of pleasure, but of *pain*.

I gripped the steel pipes above the urinal and squeezed, as the pain seared awareness of my friend in the restroom—and all other thoughts—from my brain. I hoped I wouldn't pass out. I'd been there before. Too many times. Practice gives you an instinctive awareness of where to look. Keep your eye on the penis. What comes out is all-important.

What comes out now? Chunks of fresh calves' liver. Three pieces, to be exact. The largest nearly an inch in length and spreading to half an inch in width as it plops into the urinal. Bloody pieces of my interior self flushing painfully out along with dark, dirty-looking blood. Followed by a trickle of slightly clearer liquid remotely related to urine. I haven't screamed. Or have I? I can't remember. My wrists hurt from hanging onto the pipes on the wall. Out of the corner of my eye I notice my compatriot turning away from the urinal. Did he see? Did he wonder what the hell all the trauma was about? *I don't care.* I sag against the wall. My mind fills with a multitude of thoughts, covering all aspects of the significance of this adventure. I look into the urinal. The calves' liver is still there. I pull the lever. *Flush*! (If only I had a vial of formaldehyde to preserve all that for later documentation.)

The need to pee had passed. My urinary tract burned like hell, but I felt momentarily better. I moved quickly out of the restroom and asked for help to get my plane returned to its parking spot. Montana would have to wait, for I knew I wouldn't be leaving in the morning. When I *would* be leaving I also knew I didn't know. I took myself home. What I should have known was that the worst was yet to come.

When I got home I went to bed. I remained there for three days and nights, getting up only to pass liver, blood and brown urine. At least now I had no spectators and was free to scream, *literally*, with the pain as my body continued its discharge.

I developed sores over much of my pubic area. My entire body felt like I had been beaten with baseball bats. Getting up to go to the bathroom took absolutely all the energy I had. It also involved vomiting and diarrhea for the first day or so, until there was nothing left to evacuate. The sores would come and go, only to be replaced by fresh ones. I ate nothing and drank only bancha tea with *kuzu* and *umeboshi* plum in it. I didn't sleep. After the first three days I was able to get out of bed and move around the house. I began to eat a little rice cream. It was nearly a week before I left the house.

I had plenty of time to think: it had been eight years, nearly to the day, since I first pissed blood in the spring of 1975 and began my journey of self-healing. Eight years. How long does it take for every cell in the body to be replaced? Seven or eight years (depending on age, sex and condition).

Was my cancer back? *No.* Could I now finally call myself cured? *No.* Is there such a thing as being cured? *No. No. No.* Could my prostatic tumor return? *Yes.*

The passion with which the medical establishment and general population search for a "cure" for this or that disease amazes me. Their search can't help but be in vain. It is founded on an illusion. Billions of dollars spent; thousands of poor dumb animals vivisected in research; millions of people sacrificed to chemotherapy, radiation, etc. Chasing after what they can never have, because it doesn't exist (except in the collective minds of institutionalized medicine): *freedom from disease.*

You want to be free of sickness . . . die! Death is the only real "cure" for the maladies of life. Sickness and health are the winters and summers of our lives. And with each season, with each survival of our deepest, darkest winters, we are enriched, deepened, so that we may better benefit from and enjoy the summers of this lifetime.

There is no end to this cycle in our lives until we die and pass on. This book is nothing more than a handbook for survival. How to have the life you were allotted. On your terms. We can survive all the winters, all the sicknesses; that it is our destiny, our *right* to experience. But we must do it ourselves.

Every day of my life I am asked why, if I'm so healthy, do I have a cold? Why do I have a fever? Why do I get pimples? Why do I piss blood eight years after I supposedly cured myself of cancer? The stupidity and ignorance that makes such questions possible always leaves me speechless. It so entirely misses the point—the whole point of life. I *must* get sick if I am going to continue to live. I will survive *all* my sicknesses, and I will do it my*self*! My life is my own. Nothing can kill me but my lack of judgment and understanding. The notion that there exist "incurable diseases" is as false as the one that claims the earth is flat. *We always die by our own hand.*

If you decide to follow the dietary principles in this book, that alone means nothing. You must do it yourself. Cook your own food. Take your own advice. Learn by your own mistakes. Be the captain of your own ship. Do so for seven or eight years and perhaps *then* you'll begin to get the point. Until then, keep your mouth shut! Don't join the thousands proudly announcing they've been practicing something called macrobiotics for six days, weeks, months, and gee, do they feel great. Wait! If you feel great, then you ain't doing it, brother. The path to understanding is not paved with joyous days of munching brown rice! This book is *not* fiction. Nor is it unique. Should you choose to follow the path of this Kamikaze Cowboy, you too will have a tale of countless journeys through the pain-filled valleys of self-discovery as you truly gain mastery over your life. Be patient. Be doctor. Be well.

PART FOUR

Long ago the land was ruled with a wisdom
Too fine, too deep, to be fully understood
And, since it was beyond men's full understanding,
Only some of it has come down to us, as in these sayings:
"Alert as a winter-farer on an icy stream,"
"Wary as a man in ambush,"
"Considerate as a welcome guest,"
"Selfless as melting ice,"
"Green as an uncut tree,"
"Open as a valley,"
And this one also: "Roiled as a torrent."
Why roiled as a torrent?
Because when a man is in turmoil, how shall he find peace
Save by staying patient till the stream clears?
How can a man's life keep its course
If he will not let it flow?
Those who flow as life flows know
They need no other force:
They feel no wear, they feel no tear,
They need no mending, no repair.

—Lao Tzu, *The Way of Life*
(Witter Bynner, trans.)

CHAPTER ONE

THE PROOF IS IN YOUR PEEING

I promised myself when I started writing this Kamikaze manifesto that I wouldn't give away any secrets, that any interested reader would have to discover for him or herself the way to health and happiness. If I hand it to you here in these pages, you will miss the whole point that it *must* be discovered *by* you if it is to be of any value *to* you.

But I'm going to break my promise to myself and give you this much: *The quickest, surest way to know your immediate physical condition is to examine the condition of your daily waste products.* They are the result of the food and drink you are consuming. Examine them according to color, texture, buoyancy, quantity and shape. If you pee more than three (four if you're a female) times a day, you ain't healthy. I don't care what your family witch-doctor says. If you don't defecate once a day, no more and no less, you got problems. If your fecal matter doesn't float, if it is black or green or runny or too hard, you ain't healthy. You may run ten miles a day, bench-press 400 pounds and have the tan of Tom Selleck, but you ain't healthy. You are suffering from eating habits that will sooner or later lead to more serious symptoms than unpleasant visits, or the lack thereof, to the john.

One should urinate two to four times a day, depending on age, sex and weather. The urine should be the color of light beer. Lighter or darker denotes an excess of either yin or yang food and/or drink. Solid waste should be evacuated once a day, ideally in the morning, shortly after waking up. It should be light brown and buoyant. If it is hard and shiny and/or in small, round pellet form a la Bre'r Rabbit, you better quit the animal food, salt and other overly yang tidbits. Diarrhea and constipation are totally unnatural conditions and signs of a serious imbalance in what you've been stuffing yourself with. Enemas and other such treatments are symptomatic in nature and not only do nothing to deal with the *cause*, but further aggravate the situation.

So you see, you need go no farther than your own bathroom for a daily checkup that will tell you more about your physical condition than any battery of tests at the local medical factory. And it's *free*! Conduct your private checkup, adjust your diet according to yin/yang and wait till the next day to see what happens. The proof is in your peeing.

The proof was certainly in *my* peeing! Who knew that hidden in my twenty-nine-year-old prostate, waiting to be discovered as the star of my Kamikaze epic, was an accumulation of animal fat, oil and protein in the form of a tumor? Twenty-nine, going on thirty, is a very young age to have such severe problems with your prostate. I am sure, however, that as I write this twelve years later, there are those degenerative young, the product of Big Mac parents, who have had this "old-timer's" malady at an age that makes even twenty-nine sound old! I may have had the prostate of a sixty-five-year-old, but there are now ten-year-old kids who have the entire *body* of a sixty-five-to-eighty-year-old.

The aging process is a manifestation of the metabolic rate of the human body, and that metabolism is nothing more or less than the direct reflection of the quantity and quality of food we fuel that body with. You may choose to deny the validity of this fact. I do not. The proof is in my celluloid scrapbook! As I shed the skin that beef and milk built and created new stuff from grain and vegetables, I discovered what the all-seeing eye of the cinematic camera could only assume to be "The Fountain of Youth." I have had my rebirth on film.

My prostate wasn't the only organ that was suffering from the prematurely aging effects of meat, sugar, cow milk, etc. If my career should be so kind, I may someday have to suffer through a Dirk Benedict Film Festival. What a shock it will be to *see* that the D.B. of 1971 and 1972 was years older than the D.B. of 1978! For to the eye of any beholder, I did, in fact, look seven years younger. My over-forty-year-old mug is proof that the Fountain of Youth is in those amber waves of *grain* and *not* those bloody sides of beef. The proof is in the close-up.

Just for the record, let me state what should be all too obvious to those who know me and even to those who read between these lines. I have never "taken care" of myself. My path has always been one of extremes, never knowing what was enough until I'd had *more* than enough. Even in my application of yin/yang I overdid it. With total disregard for my body (partly out of ignorance, partly out of the love of risk, partly out of an overly abundant curiosity and impatience), I went too far in every direction until no matter how correct that direction was, it turned into its opposite, and I took three steps backwards. I was the rat in my experiment.

How just it would be if all the mad scientists in modern medical laboratories around the country were forced to use themselves, instead of God's unsuspecting creatures, as guinea pigs for their insane experiments to test their "theories" (euphemism for guesses) as to what causes cancer, diabetes, M.S., Alzheimer's, etc. Leave the rabbits and mice and monkeys out of it, poor dumb creatures that they are.

Try it on yourself, baby. Consider the fact that we are all, in a larger sense, simply guinea pigs in the laboratories of these same scientists and their corporate medical machines as they inflict hundreds of substances upon our bodies, unsure of what effect they have on the living human organism. Not a month goes by that you don't read in the paper or see on *60 Minutes* the disclosure of yet another additive or medicine that has been "discovered" to cause cancer in human tissue. "Oops! Sorry, folks, not enough testing was done."

Try it on yourself, doctor, and get back to me in three or four months. That's what I did. We should go back to the ways of the ancient Chinese: family doctors were paid only as long as the family stayed healthy. When a person became sick, the doctor's payment ceased until he cured his patient. Do you pay your auto mechanic for failing to fix your engine's misfiring? Only doctors. The spell they hold over the American public is beyond belief.

Go to the supermarket. Read the labels. And despair. All those long, multisyllabic words are potential killers waiting for validation by the lemming-like masses of America as they dash madly towards a carcinogenic sea. Not me. Try it on yourself, doctor, and get back to me. Meanwhile, if it ain't whole and holy, born of the same soil to which I shall return and become food myself, I ain't buying. The only insanity to which I will be subjected is my own.

To this day, in answer to those who accuse me of being a health nut, I point out that I smoke three or four cigars a day and occasionally indulge in a myriad of practices, all of which would not, in anybody's book, come under the heading of health-oriented. Which is not to say I am not healthy. The very phrase "health nut" I find rather amusing. If a person concerned with improving the quality of his or her physical/spiritual life is a "health nut," does this mean that a person not bothered with such concerns, who eats at random with chaos and ignorance as his or her only guide, is a "sickness nut"? You out there, are you all sickness nuts?

The point isn't whether you smoke or drink or eat meat or chew gladiola petals; the point is *why* you make the choices you do. What is the method to your particular madness? In the all-encompassing world of yin and yang, there are times when meat and sugar would be just the ticket! Ask a "vegetarian" (will someone *please* define that word for me?)

sometime to explain the pristine health of the native Alaskan. The Eskimo's natural diet before white men invaded with sugar, etc., was almost entirely composed of food from animal and fish sources. If animal fat and oil are by their very nature inherently *bad*, then how could these people have had a quality of health unsurpassed by any contemporary Alaskan resident? A meatless meanderer who spends any time in the frozen north will very soon become ill and eventually succumb unless he adjusts what he eats to the environment into which he has meandered!

We all have to eat. It is the most overpowering and obvious common denominator of mankind. There isn't a profession, an event, an activity, an occasion that doesn't include *food. Food is life.* Food is the great variable that shapes history. Name any endeavor that involves human beings and food is a part of it: marriage, sporting events, hunting parties, war meetings, peace conferences. There is no plan for the achievement of any goal that doesn't include food. And it is food that is the key as to whether that plan is a success. Ask Columbus, Admiral Peary, Hilary, Capt. John Smith, Hitler, Hannibal, Westmoreland. Ask any Viet Nam vet who fought the Vietnamese in their own rice paddies. Without food, nothing succeeds.

When someone wants to convince others of the rightness of his particular cause, and all other means of conversion have failed, what does that person always resort to? Fasting! When someone gives up what no one can live without, it communicates on a level that cuts through all the talking, conferring, warring. Food is life.

Because we must all have it, there is the tragic assumption we must all have it in the same way. We assume that food is food; when you're hungry, eat. It's only important *not* to be hungry. Our choices of what we eat are based eighty percent of the time on what is nearest at hand when we decide we're hungry. The other twenty percent of the time, we eat according to emotional, sentimental and/or intellectual reasons. Gourmets . . . seeking ever more stimulating treats to tantalize taste buds that have long ago lost their ability to recognize truth. Taste buds that have been so inundated with an array of different taste "treats" that they are always in need of ever more extreme sensations in order to taste anything at all.

Then there are the people who need the emotional fix of dining in a restaurant with just the right decor, lighting and stroking by the maitre d'. Nothing to do with the cause and effect of what it is they are actually ingesting in their cozy, comfy, candlelit gastronomic boudoir. Sentimentalists in constant search of the next "in" restaurant.

There is another group of people who eat for reasons other than the mere fact that they are hungry. It is to this group that the overeducated of America flock in ever-growing numbers. Educated beyond all innate ability to think for themselves, they fall prey to whatever the latest fad is in eating a "balanced diet"! They go from one diet fashion to the next, depending upon which book is on the NY *Times* Best-Seller List, which tennis or movie star or ex-president's wife is promoting her/his secret-to-success/beauty diet. All-protein diets, no-protein diets, all-fruit diets, cottage-cheese-and-strawberries diets, no-salt diets, low-salt diets, high-fat and no-fat diets, high-carbohydrate diets, diets with roughage, without roughage, with fish, without fish, diets with nothing but carrot juice except on the fourth day of every week unless there's an "R" in the month and then the fifth day of every other week except for Leos, who should never have carrot juice until their Sun is in Pluto and their daughter's in trouble.

This is no joke. I even heard of a diet which had the person eating a different fruit each day of the week: Monday, nothing but grapes; Tuesday, watermelon; Wednesday, pomegranates, etc., etc. Nothing surprises me anymore.

All these diets fail for one very simple reason. They are *man-made*. They cannot be followed for a lifetime, so when one goes off the diet, what happens? Right back to their previous condition. They are all temporary treatments of symptoms, dietary bandaids. All different manifestations of our attempts to find a "better," "healthier" way of feeding ourselves. Ignorant of the natural laws of order that govern *everything*, including (especially) what we choose as our food.

If you ever see a book whose author proclaims he has discovered *The Perfect Diet*, forget it; if you've already bought it, burn it. He's a fool making money off other fools' misguided attempts to have what is already theirs by the very nature of their *being*.

But what of *this* book, you ask? If you do, you have missed the whole point, for although it may be many things, cover many numbers in the Dewey Decimal System, the one thing it *isn't* is a *diet* book. It may be a "how-to" book, a "way-of-life" book, but never diet, for there are no laws, do's and don't's, merely principles by which we can regain what we have lost: freedom from all dietary rules and regulations.

Study your yin and yang. The question is not what you eat, but *why*. Every person is unique, infinitely unique by virtue of his or her inherited constitution, age, sex, occupation, environment (is he or she building igloos or bamboo huts?), etc. And according to all these variables, your diet will be unique unto you. And if you are healthy, if your instincts are alive and well (unlikely in this day and age), you will fulfill this unique diet by simply eating what you *want*. And what you want will be what you need. And the proof will be in the peeing.

CHAPTER TWO

WE ALL SCREAM FOR ICE CREAM

Not too long ago on the ABC *Nightly News*, Peter Jennings reporting, it was stated that the *latest* medical research had discovered that salt is *not* the cause of high blood pressure. Are you listening to this? They are saying that all those low-sodium diets, all those lectures by your doctor on the evils of salt, might be wrong! Jennings went on to report findings that indicate that a salt-free or low-sodium diet is *not* advised for those with high blood pressure. What is needed to combat high blood pressure and hypertension, they said, are trace minerals. Like calcium. Now we all know, from our sixth-grade class on nutrition, where America gets its calcium: *dairy food.* And guess who funded all this research into the role of salt and the need for calcium in our diets? That's right . . . the *American Dairy Association*!

The spokesman for the report assured us that their findings were in no way influenced by the fact that the dairy association was the money behind their research program. Dissenting medical opinions were, of course, offered. The segment ended with the recommendation that you should continue following your doctor's advice if you have been suffering from blood-pressure-related problems. Everybody's ass was covered.

Listen to the doctor, don't listen to the doctor. Less salt, more salt. More calcium, no calcium. Are you confused? Do you wish there was another way to go? Available to all? If after reading this book, you can't see it, go see your doctor. You deserve him.

This particular story is but one of scores you can find every day of your life by reading a newspaper or two or watching the morning and evening news programs. We are a nation obsessed with what we are rapidly bankrupting ourselves of . . . *health*. The situation is desperate.

Forget what your doctor tells you . . . just look around. Start with yourself. How do you feel? How do your wife, your kids, your parents, your neighbors, your working associates *feel*? How do they look? How many people do you know who aren't overweight? America is *fat*! That's why we are preoccupied with being thin. The point of mentioning the little news item is merely to suggest that you had better stop trusting your doctor! Doctors are *fat*. Fat inside and out. Fat people with fat lifestyles. What they are good at is mending broken bones, sewing up torn skin, *not* treating the *cause* of our disease.

Ever consider how many hundreds of millions of dollars are made by selling various food items labeled ''salt-free''? There are entire sections of supermarkets marked ''low sodium.'' You can get anything without salt, including salt. Salt-free salt. Salt for people who can't eat salt. Think how devastating it would be to this big business if all of a sudden it was discovered that what we *really* need are *high-salt* diets! ''High-sodium'' sections would spring up in your local supermarket faster than you can say ''market research.''

Read your newspapers. The Dairy Association is nervous. The truth about milk, cheese, etc., is beginning to be found out. Arthritis, allergies, obesity, excess mucus, etc., etc., are all being linked to too much moo juice. ''Everybody may *not* need milk!'' There's one thing you can be absolutely sure of and that is: The food conglomerates of this country do not package, market and sell food to promote health, they do it to make *money*! I don't care what they say in their reports, their advertisements, their medically sanctioned findings proclaiming the credibility of their products . . . it's all Madison Avenue hype, medicine avenue doubletalk orchestrated to get you, the frightened, confused public, to *buy their product*. And you do!

We all drink mother's milk as long as that holds out, and then we turn to mama cow with relish and suck at her udder for a lifetime. All to the financial glee of Darigold, Hansen's, Borden, etc. It's no accident that we never grow up when we eat the food of children our entire lives. Even mama cow knows when it's time for her youngster to grow up and forsake her udder for a pile of hay. Not humans. Grown men and women sitting down to their milkshakes, yogurt and cottage cheese. ''Baby food'' in every possible sense of the term.

Ask anybody, the most difficult kind of food to forsake is dairy food. Now that it is in vogue and has become the diet of the stars, how eager everyone is to let you know they no longer eat meat, that they are ''vegetarians'' (whatever the hell that word means). But follow them through one of their days and you'll be dumbfounded at the amount of animal food they consume. All in the form of dairy products.

Give me liberty or give me death, but good God almighty, don't take away my milk and cookies! How cozy to curl up in front of Johnny Carson with a warm glass of hot cocoa after a brutal day in the workaday world. Solace, comfort, slipping back into our babyhood. Sucking at the nipple of our erstwhile mamma.

Melt cheese on anything and people will eat it. I've been to many four-star restaurants whose world-famous chefs refuse to serve their specialty of the evening if you won't allow them to melt cheese over it. To what cooking school does one need to go to learn to do that?

The damage done to the human organism by all this consumption of bovine juice still goes unpublicized. Sure, it causes allergies in some people; it does form mucus; arthritis has been known to go away when you stop consuming it; stomach problems have subsided when it is given up. But all in all, it is still considered "America's drink." Every*body* needs it. Never mind the cow-like bodies of the men and women who consume it. The "saddlebags" women pay millions of dollars to have pounded, whacked and cut from their legs are the direct result of their "lo-cal fix" of dairy delight. But don't try to tell them that. Don't try to tell them that what everybody *doesn't* need is milk!

CHAPTER THREE

TYRANNY OF THE INVALIDS

Examine yourself. Are you already a bonafide member of that expanding segment of society that practices its tyranny on a rapidly dwindling group of truly healthy individuals? If so, beware! Who will pay your social security, medicare, insurance premiums? Who will raise the millions for your intricate, expensive life-support systems? Who will push your wheelchairs?

 INTEROFFICE MEMORANDUM

Date   FEBRUARY 22, 1984

To   GEORGE, DIRK, MR. T., DWIGHT

From   STEVE SASSEN

ON FRIDAY, FEBRUARY 24, 1984, SAMANTHA
AND HER PARENTS WOULD LIKE TO COME TO THE SET
TO BRIEFLY VISIT WITH THE A-TEAM. SAMANTHA
HAS BONE CANCER AND HER DREAM IS TO VISIT THE
SET.

THANKS,

cc: J. Ashley
   D. Birnie
   C. Clay
   K. Foster
   J. Pare'
   C. West
   G. Brown

We have become a nation that caters to the unhealthy. How sad. How frightening. The healthy are made to pay the way for the ever-increasing number of people at ever-increasingly younger ages who are incapable of caring for themselves.

As a member of *The A-Team*, I was in a wonderful position to observe this growing tyranny of the invalids. It was the wish of millions of kids throughout this country to visit the set of *The A-Team*, to meet Mr. T, Hannibal, Howling Mad Murdock, Faceman. As is true of all hit TV shows, ours was a set that was very hard to gain access to. There are many reasons for this. Most of them are simply a matter of practicality. The filming of a show such as ours involved lots of action, a very tight schedule and long, tiring hours; it could have been easily disrupted by visitors innocently asking for autographs or standing in the wrong place at the wrong time. I would have been hesitant to have my own niece and nephew visit, knowing what a disruption it was, what an energy drain for cast and crew to have strangers hanging about. And it was a hazardous environment. Innocent bystanders could have gotten hurt. We simply *did not allow visitors*!

Most of *The A-Team* was shot on location in and around the sprawling metropolis of Los Angeles. Needless to say, we were often surrounded by kids wanting to get a glimpse of their heroes. People were hired to make sure that such kids not only didn't get close enough for an autograph and/or photograph, but that they didn't even get close enough for their desperate *living* wish for a glimpse. We *paid* people to make sure that didn't happen.

But nonetheless, we did have visitors! Can you guess from what segment of the populace they came? That's right, the sick and dying. That it was every kid's wish to see *The A-Team* in action was understandable, but we couldn't do anything about it, nor did we try. It was too much to ask.

However, when that wish was the *dying* wish of a child, he had immediate access to Mr. T's private motor home.

So there was an endless stream of the sick and dying youth of America through the healthy, active life of *The A-Team*. Wanna meet Mr. T? Get a doctor's affadavit confirming your terminal case of leukemia. We had 'em all: diabetes, leukemia, cancer of every kind, some with names so long and obscure that only a Johns Hopkins graduate could pronounce them. There is even a television program (only in America!) that caters to the dying wishes of young kids around the country, making money by fulfilling their last requests on this earth. Many of these last gasps at life were spent seeing Hannibal, B.A., Murdock and What's-his-Face in action up close and personal. They *always* got what they wished.

So, did you wanna get your wish fulfilled? You just got sick, *really* sick . . . and if the TV show couldn't handle your case, you just sent your dying wish, along with a doctor's stamp of verification, to the producers of *The A-Team* and you too would be having lunch with the stars. Tyranny of the invalids.

When these poor hapless dying kids visited, surrounded by their Whitman's Sampler of medical and paramedical support systems, what did they get for lunch? Diet soda, ice cream, chocolate cake, hamburgers. The perfect "Last Supper" for those condemned to try again in another lifetime.

Degeneration is beginning to manifest itself at younger and younger ages. I am continually saddened as I stand on any street corner in any city and watch the "normal" young kids of America today. It appalls me to see teenage girls running on the beach in the summer with cellulite betraying the health they seem to portray. Young boys with rolls of fat, breasts like girls, with asthma, allergies, etc. Encased in mountains of fat, they munch their french fries, guzzle their soft drinks, smoke their dope, incapable of climbing a flight of stairs without pausing to catch their breath. A grotesque reflection of the rapidly degenerative results of the eating habits of America. Imagine them in ten years, for the older you get, the more you personify what you eat.

If you've read more than one or two pages of this macrobiological autobiography, I think you can understand my state of mind at having my picture taken with an eight-year-old Leukemia victim as he sips his can of Coca-Cola. I know leukemia is curable, and the first step is to throw away the Coca-Cola and all the other things that were the *reason* for the disease in the first place.

Experience has taught me to keep my mouth shut. But finally, I'd had enough of this parade, this grotesque exercise in futile, sentimental catering to disease. I could no longer watch all those sad children, the hapless, hopeless victims of American dietary habits. I had had enough. It was time for equal time!

For every unhealthy kid who was granted entry into the hallowed bullet-ridden atmosphere of *The A-Team*, I wanted a healthy kid to be given the same rights of visitation. The publicist who organized all this thought I was joking.

"What's the point?" she asked me. "There's certainly nothing newsworthy in *healthy* kids visiting the set."

"Maybe not," I replied, "but perhaps there's *something* to be gained."

If *The A-Team* was about anything, as it struggled to entertain the folks across America, it was about people standing up for themselves against the imposition of will by those who would have them do other than what they want. Standing up against oppression. Having control of your own life. *The A-Team* was available to help anybody stand up to those "bad guys" who wouldn't allow them to live their lives as they chose to. When the villains tried to control others, in swooped *The A-Team* to make sure it didn't happen. Four guys all rolled up into one persona . . . one superman on the side of good. Well, that wasn't too bad a premise for a weekly television show. I wouldn't mind having *my* kid watch people representing such values.

So, I explained to the publicist that if *The A-Team* was to have any real value, it was only to the extent that kids relate to this premise. And it would take healthy kids. The hope of America is in its children. It always has been, and I wanted the *healthy* kids of America to have the same chances as the unhealthy. It bothered me no end to see some bright-eyed, bouncy kid of eight pushed out of the way by a hired bodyguard to make way for a wheelchair. Tyranny of the invalids.

We cannot let *sickness* become fashionable, vogue, chic. Madison Avenue will make it just that when the numbers warrant it. When a large enough segment of the consuming public has cancer, rest assured Big Business will find a way to make money out of it.

Hell, even my grandmother knew that "health is the one thing money can't buy." But the American Cancer Society and all those tennis-playing celebrities disagree with her as they load up on roast beef, Diet Coke and ice cream between sets. All in the name of sickness. So it is no small accident that *The A-Team*, a show that exuded energy and derring-do in the face of danger, was a prime target for all those individuals and organizations out to promote their particular group of the sick and dying.

Grandma was right: "Without your health, you have nothing." As with the individual, so also with a nation: when its people's health is bankrupt, there *is* no future. Invalidated by the invalids.

CHAPTER FOUR

COLLEGE OF FOOLS

Like everyone else, I was told regularly that without a college degree, my future was hopeless. My four years of academia were a constant struggle to remain hopeful and happy in spite of the gross, eerily unnatural pressures to achieve an ever-better grade-point average. It became almost impossible to have any *fun*!

I was told time and again I wasn't in college to have fun, but to get an education. My little voice, meanwhile, told me that if you couldn't have fun doing something, then it wasn't worth doing . . . an axiom I follow much more completely today than I did back in college in the 1960s. (Of course, I do make exceptions, as exemplified by the writing of this book.) I'm so grateful that I survived and did have fun while getting "programmed" to fit into American society. Yes, it cost me in the grade-point average department, but ask me if it ruined my life. Ask me if I've ever been asked for proof that I have a college degree. Ask me what I remember most about the four years I spent getting an education. Ask yourself, all you college graduates: how much of the "information" you crammed into your skulls do you remember? History, psychology, economics, chemistry, biology . . . how much of all that data can you recall, and how has it improved for you the quality of this lifetime's experience?

If you possess a college education—have your Bachelor's, your Master's, your Doctorate—and question the wisdom of these words . . . why are you reading this book? The fact that you paid your hard-earned money for this little volume is proof of the desperate situation you find yourself in and of the fantastic success of the spiritual killing you have been submitted to as you denied your "little voice" within and plugged into the "expert" advice of the professionals. You have been "educated" into a state of ignorance. Ignorance of the real magic that should be the driving force in all our lives.

I was lucky. I survived the educational holocaust to which every able-bodied child in this country is subjected. I hung on desperately to my little voice within whispering encouragement, as time and again I went against the knowledgeable advice of my peers, pals, teachers, doctors, lawyers, coaches, lovers, all of whom predicted failure, disappointment and unhappiness for not following their heartfelt and sometimes "expert" advice.

If you didn't have fun while you struggled to get those grades, cram for those tests, you wasted all those moments in this lifetime, and they will never come again! The truth is that no one ever became rich (if that was your motivation for gaining ever more bits of information) from the number of degrees they possess. I'm rich. I'm famous. And believe me, it had nothing to do with having a college degree.

You want fame? You want fortune? Nurture your imagination, your intangible ability to dream and your constitutional strength, with which you can turn those flights of fantasy into *reality*. Have *fun*!

The ability to do all this begins first and foremost in what you choose to feed your total self . . . your body, your brain, your spirit. Sickness is disharmony, imbalance. All diseases are the result of the body trying to create harmony and balance in its blood stream out of disharmony and imbalance. When the imbalance results from a lack, we must acquire what we lack. When it is the result of excess, we must discharge that excess.

My excess was meat. That I always craved carbohydrates and bread is no mere quirk of nature. My constant eating of animal protein, salt and fat left my body trying to maintain a balance in the protein/carbohydrate ratio and in the sodium/potassium ratio. When bread wouldn't satisfy this imbalance,

I would crave beer, then sugar, and finally, though I never got to that, drugs: things ever more and more yin in their function.

Yin versus yang. Expansion versus contraction. Simple, right? Yes, if you believe and study. No, if you are arrogant and don't study. Yes, if you are possessed of strong instincts and common sense. No, if you are an educated intellectual immersed in the abstract theories of Western scientific thought.

Macrobiotics is much too simplistic for the supremely educated, knowledgeable, ever-analyzing ways of Western man's approach to the life experience. He knows life is "logical," rational. If A equals B, and B equals C, it follows then that A equals C. And in his blind belief in this sensible, explainable way of living his life, he is constantly cursing his "bad luck" that things don't turn out the way they are supposed to. According to the syllogism. Despair. Bitterness. An ever-growing feeling of frustration and anger at his inability to "control" life, predict his destiny, his lot in this lifetime.

And the more he analyzes, the more he frantically attempts to control each situation, the more he has his hopes and dreams shattered. Shattered by a force much larger than his intellect, much more powerful than his will. For example, how arrogant is man to think that by damming the Missouri River he can control it! Momentarily, perhaps, for a decade or a hundred years, but whatever has a front has a back. Eventually the river will brush away all of man's attempts to control it and recarve its natural channels back to the ocean, fulfilling an infinite design that whoever built such an atrocity as a concrete dam was incapable of comprehending. And when the dam bursts, how horror-struck we are! How cruel is life! As if there were no reason for it.

We never stop to consider that cancer, like a bursting dam, is a result of man's attempt to control that which will be forever beyond his control. Hence his inability to live in harmony with the omnipotent powers of the infinite universe.

Get this: *Cancer is a desperate attempt on the part of Mother Nature to get us to let go*, quit sinning, transgressing against the holy order of the universe. It is a disease of the spirit as well as the body. For spirit and matter are not two, but one.

But how arrogant we are, and consequently how rich the ever-growing number of psychiatrists and medical doctors. All offering a multitudinous number of ways to dam up the river of our life's natural channel as it flows through this lifetime and on into infinity. How our ego insists on taking all the blame and therefore, all the credit.

It would be far better for us to cease the excesses, the horrendous crimes against nature, that result from our inability to become part of this natural order of the universe. Uncle Harry's prostate cancer is God's reminder to him that he has sinned against the order of the universe. He eats too much rich animal food, and this selfish consumption of more than is rightfully his manifests itself not only in his prostate but in every level of his life. Accumulation of excess. Imbalance. If he changes, he is forgiven; the prostate will return to normal. It is so simple.

If Uncle Harry doesn't change the way he eats, he will die of prostate cancer. Nature will out. If the United States doesn't change its eating habits, there will be a nuclear holacaust and we will die on a global scale. Nature will have its way. The river will return to the channel bed it chooses. The planet earth will only stand for so much pollution. As a nation we will go through what I went through on the island of Leros, Greece. That was my personal holocaust. The violent explosion of a being changing direction.

Out of that explosion began a golden era in my life and the real fulfillment of my manifest destiny without the necessity for me to "control" its direction. I am not afraid of what appears to be more and more inevitable. Worldwide nuclear warfare. I have already let go. And indeed (even the Bible says so), there will be those who survive. On what basis will they be the chosen ones? Will it perhaps be the degree to which they are living their lives as part of, not separate from, the divine order of the universe? If so, the chosen will not include the filet mignon-peach cobbler-chocolate sundae crowd who attend church every Sunday, any more than Uncle Harry's filet mignon-peach cobbler-chocolate sundae-induced cancer can be cured by chemotherapy or prayer.

The idea that what sits on that plate before us decides not only the physical, mental and spiritual health of our individual selves, but also of our families, our communities, our nations and our planet, is too simple, too profit-proof. No one wants to believe that food can cure our body's illnesses. How impossible for them to believe that the spiritual illness that grips the planet and has us all on the brink of nuclear devastation could be just as simply cured.

Years ago, when I mentioned that I was going to cure my physical problems with food, I was laughed out of every conversation in which the subject was broached. When I say that the sickness of worldwide nuclear armament is a direct reflection of a planet of people individually sick but curable by food, I am likewise laughed at.

How seriously are the judgmental qualities of the brain affected by hardening of the arteries, hypoglycemia, diabetes? Let me put it this way: I'm a private pilot . . . I wouldn't get in an airplane with a sugar junky at the controls. It is *illegal* to fly an airplane unless at least eight hours have passed since your last cocktail. In my opinion that F.A.A. regulation should be amended to include "since your last Twinkie!"

In flying an airplane, driving a car, living a life, survival is directly dependent on your ability to *react*. How good are your reflexes? And if they are good enough, is it possible to react to imminent disaster *before* it happens? How close does oncoming tragedy have to be before you take evasive action? Your reflexes are a result of the health of your total being, and your health, the quality of your intuitive reflexive reaction to all of life's stimuli, is dependent upon what you feed your human mechanism. And what you feed yourself is directly related to the extent you live your life in accord with the universal laws of nature.

Does it bother you that those powerful world leaders sitting around the summit conference table deciding the future of the planet Earth are counting the minutes till lunch and their fix of brandy, ice cream or jelly beans? Does the fate of mankind hang in the balance of some president or premier or chairman's blood-sugar count?

Frightening, right? If we as a civilization cannot bring peace and harmony, health and happiness into this world, then it will be done for us. If we cannot stop drinking a fifth of vodka a day, then it will be done for us. If our egos, our overly aggressive behavior, our schizophrenic mentalities, our winning-is-everything nationalistic consciousness are not changed *by* us . . . they will be changed *for* us. Nuclear devastation. And then perhaps the beginning of a Golden Age.

If only two, one man and one woman, survive, it will be a Golden Age to be enjoyed by them, their children and their children's children. And nature will begin again. In the divine scheme of things, it doesn't matter which way it happens.

With our attachment to this life and its importance—our two cars, stereo systems, color TVs, two-week vacations, complicated support systems—we fear death because it means *no more* to us. A letting go. No more MacDonald's hamburgers. No more NBC. No more golf.

In *truth* all of that is an illusion, a dream which we will all have to let go of eventually anyway. And all the political, socioeconomic, nationalistic reasons for nuclear armament are likewise illusions, fantasies. Nightmares dreamed by a diseased mankind. The alarm clock that awakens us may be nuclear powered.

This Kamikaze Cowboy's dream is of another way. I have let go; I am joyous and grateful for this life and all its myriad pleasures, but it is not the reason for my existence. I have let go.

CHAPTER FIVE

YOU'RE ON YOUR OWN

The other day, as I was wending my way toward the set of *The A-Team*, I was reminded yet again of how unnecessary this book really is. It was early in the morning and the beginning of another hectic day of trying to do in twelve hours what needs twenty-four to accomplish. As usual, the set was surrounded with onlookers. Out of the mish-mash of unknown faces I heard my name called.

This isn't an unusual occurrence for anyone caught in a state of celebrity. Acting may be the only profession in which, no matter how involved you are in doing your job, perfect strangers feel no compunction about coming up and interrupting you, requesting an autograph, a handshake or to tell you they "know who you are."

No matter what your profession is, consider for a moment what it would be like to try to perform your duties while being constantly interrupted, to be stopped continually for idle conversation, pointless chit-chat, as you struggle to do whatever it is you do to make a living. But in the acting profession you're fair game and it's open season all year long, twenty-four hours a day. Consequently, the need to be able to tell when the person demanding your time and energy is worthwhile, or when he/she is a waste of your time and energy, becomes of paramount importance.

In this instance I immediately recognized that whoever was calling my name had something very specific to share with me. I turned, as the quality of the voice hooked my attention, and saw the person responsible. He was standing behind the bulk of the crowd, leaning against one of the dressing-room trailers. Instinctually, I walked straight toward him.

I didn't recognize him as someone I should know. But nonetheless, I knew him. We shared a common bond. Like the veterans of Viet Nam who struggled to stay alive in the endless rice paddies of the nightmare that only they could truly comprehend, we needed no dialogue to share the experience we had in common. Words were unnecessary because I could see him, hear him and touch him as I reached out to shake his hand.

It was then he said, "You don't remember me, do you?"

I didn't. But this was not so much a comment on my memory as on the transformation he had undergone.

"I used to be your agent."

In my haphazard, avocational career I've had *many* agents, but I remembered this man's name. And I remembered that he had been my first agent upon my re-entry into Hollywood after my cancer-induced sabbatical.

Shortly after I came back into town with the goal of finishing the Hollywood part of my life and completing a cycle I had started with *Chopper One*, I was invited to a party by a former member of the cast of that ill-fated series. It was at this party that I was approached by a fellow who said he'd like to represent me. At that time he was a man of medium build who weighed about 150 pounds.

Now, as we spoke these lifetimes later on the *A-Team* set, I asked him "How much weight have you lost?"

"Thirty pounds."

"Not as much as me," I told him. But then I'd had more excess to shed, more sins to atone for. "On what part of your body did you discover it?"

He pointed to his kidney area.

How he took me back to myself when I was in the middle of my self-treatment! All skin and bone. No fat and damn little muscle. Only what was necessary to get around.

We spoke for only a few minutes. Time is money, as they say, and it was never more apropos than on a television show, where a minute is worth about $200! And anyway, like all people who have lived through the same experience, in which death is a distinct possibility, words were really unimportant. We understood.

His story was nearly a carbon copy of my own, as mine was of hundreds before me: the recognition of the disease; the awareness of an alternative approach; the escape from the hands of those who wanted him to submit to traditional forms of treatment—chemotherapy, surgery, etc.; his decision to apply the principles of yin/yang and become responsible for his own life and his own death; the myriad of changes he was going through, that I went through, that everyone goes through who changes the quality of their blood in order to regain harmony and balance and health. It is a journey that never ends, as he told me he was just beginning to realize.

"I want to thank you," he said.

"For what? I've done nothing."

But he'd never forgotten being around me those few months when he had been my agent and had witnessed first hand what I was. We never discussed macrobiotics during those months. I certainly never tried to convert him. But he never forgot what I *was*, what I manifested.

We had had, as all agents and actors do, lunch together. That is, he ate and I explained that I was following a way of eating that didn't include the fish or meat or eggs that are the basis of luncheon fare in America. I told him I had recently recovered from cancer through self-treatment, against all the advice of those who knew my situation. So, when his carcinogenic number came up, as it does for nearly one out of every four Americans, he remembered me and the "feeling" he had had about what I had done.

So he just wanted to say thanks and express his appreciation for what he now realized I was going through. He too had now become a stranger in his own country. America and its meat-eating mentality were becoming more and more foreign to him every day: the restaurants he couldn't eat in; the supermarkets he couldn't shop in; conversations he no longer fit into; dreams he no longer shared.

Nowadays, there are restaurants that serve *whole* food, supermarkets that sell fundamental foodstufs and people such as myself who understand. But ten years ago a Kamikaze Cowboy had to carry his bag of brown rice, container of tamari and pouch of miso around with him. Or he could fast and wait for the next oasis.

"But the times, they are a-changing," I assured my former agent.

I had no choice but to learn how to prepare my own medicine. Now we go to a restaurant and hire someone to cook for us. The cycle then begins again, and we are at the mercy of whoever is doing the cooking. Yes, the times are changing, but beware, because for every front there is a back, a downside, of equal size. The more places there are to go out and eat, the less need there is to learn how to cook yourself. And it is paramount that we all learn to cook the food that will become us and fuel the realization of our dreams.

As I watched the skinny frame of my former agent saunter off, it was I who felt immense gratitude. All of the thoughts I have shared with you here, and many, many more that lie beyond my ability to express, I had during our brief encounter. How grateful I was for being reminded . . . and for being taught, once again, that it is not ourselves who decide who will and will not be affected by our lives. *People decide their own fate.* There have been loved ones, family, friends with whom I invested enormous amounts of time and energy trying to share what I have discovered in my journey toward health and happiness. All to no avail, no matter how hard I tried. Those who have been affected by my experience have always been those to whom I devoted the least of my self, and in most instances people I was unaware of having communicated with at all.

EPILOGUE

We never know the true reason why we do anything until long after we have done it. But we *always think* we know the reason. Being incredibly intelligent, rational beings, we can give lists of bonafide reasons for any life action we take, only to discover (if we are awake enough) that the influence such an action has on our life is entirely other than what we thought. ''From out of left field'' is how we describe something we hadn't thought of or planned for.

I went to New Hampshire to rid my body of cancerous degeneration centered in my prostate gland. A week after being there my prostate was the last thing on my mind. *Nothing* was on my mind. I was absorbed in the experience of the incredible changes I was going through. I now think of it as the culmination of my first thirty years. Those thirty years being a period of gestation and the six weeks in New Hampshire my birthing.

Being born into an adult body is a jolt to the psyche you cannot believe. Imagine if during your original birth you had had the awareness you processed as a thirty-year-old adult. It would be almost too much to withstand. It caught *me* by surprise.

Wanting to trade in my prematurely old prostate for a rejuvenated one, I ended up trading the entire vehicle for a completely remodeled version. *Everything* changed. This was a creeping sensation; only with time could I discuss, or in any way verbalize, the experience. And, of course, it was only the beginning of a rebirthing process that continued with some intensity for four more years and is only now, twelve years later, in its more subtle stages.

Only now am I finally a living organism founded and fueled with food from the vegetable kindgom. Only now is all of me—the quality of my hair, texture of my skin, tone of my muscles, pulse of my heart, pressure of my blood, wavelength of my brain, count of my sperm, color of my feces, aroma of my perspiration, sodium/potassium ratio of my cells, clarity of my lungs, quantity of my urine, and on and on into the farthest reaches of my being (beyond even what modern science and their omnipotent microscopic techniques can see)—completely reborn. The cabin in New Hampshire was my womb, the twelve years since have been my adolescence. This book is part of my passage into another stage. A cycle in which I must no longer discuss, explain and/or defend what I am and how I survived what is killing America by the thousands. A period in my life when I can enjoy productively the health and happiness I've been reborn into. And so richly deserve.

Today, fifteen years since quitting animal food and since my "Greek initiation rites"; fourteen years since "discovering" grains as my main food; eleven years since beginning personal treatment of my prostate tumor, I am still ridding myself of pieces of old "self" created during my first twenty-six years and by the countless generations from whose multitudinous loins I sprang.

Eating your way beyond *generation* upon generation of meat-eaters is no easy task. To assume it can be accomplished in *one* lifetime is an assumption bordering on megalomania. It is one of the great errors made by those who play around with diets to effect change in their lives, usually on the purely cosmetic level. They are completely oblivious to the awesome ramifications involved in changing what they eat. And when that change is as dramatic as going from a diet based on

animal protein, fish and fowl to grains, beans and vegetables
. . . hang on to your aura!

As I continue, every year involves the revelation of another
ghost in my dietary past. As time goes on, the change goes
deeper and deeper into the body, until finally it is happening at a cellular level and, as spirit and matter are not separate
but *one*, the "self" of yourself begins to shift. These changes
in your spiritual "self" are equally as devastating as the earlier
physical, emotional and intellectual ones.

If you don't believe the soul exists or that it can be
touched, try eating brown rice for seven years. If you were
to do so, I am sure you would wonder why I bothered to
write these words, understanding that they can only be understood by those who have been there. And, of course, those
few souls have no need to read what they already *know*. But
alas, such is my downfall.

I consider quite often the past twelve years, during which
I was on my Kamikaze way, often living a life without the
pleasures and excitements my contemporaries were enjoying:
the parties, the fancy food, the general excess that is available to all America and especially to the WWII baby-boom
generation. We were born into an affluence that few people in the history of the world have known. That any of us
have survived it to any degree is testament to the incredible
resilience of the human body/spirit. My friends and peers *did*
while I *did without.*

I am now contacted directly and indirectly by hundreds of
those people, moving into their late thirties, early forties,
wondering where it all went. Where all the health and joy
and exuberance went. And where the arthritis, the migraines,
the back problems, the obesity, the cancer (ah yes, the cancer)
in every organ of their bodies, the baldness, the lack of vitality, the constipation, all came *from*. This book is my open
answer to all of them.

How well I know the phantasmagoria of delights they

were tempted with as they danced, smoked, tooted and dropped their way into the sixties and seventies. If the twenties were "roaring," the sixties were cyclonic! The Cyclonic Sixties . . . a decade in which America reached the point of no return.

We are degenerating at such a rapid rate now that I think the time has already come when it is very difficult to find a single human being who isn't in a precarcinogenic or prediabetic state. We have all become walking time bombs for which only years will be necessary for us to explode in a physiological devastation that will leave America a nation of sick and dying. We will all be in the same (sinking) boat. And whatever show is the hit of America's airwaves then will have a cast consisting of one diabetic, one leukemia victim, one triple bypass and one kidney dialysis patient. Who will visit that set as a part of their dying wish? What healthy individual will want to rub shoulders with such "stars"? How far from present-day reality is such a situation? How many of our nation's heroes are hypoglycemic, diabetic, alcoholic, cocaine addicts, valium addicts, aspirin addicts, Coca-Cola addicts? Junkies, one and all. And in our ignorance and gluttony, we are surprised, shocked, to read of yet another "healthy" young athlete dead from an overdose, or a president's wife hooked on drugs.

How healthy is healthy? How many people do you know who don't get a cold at least once a year? Who have headaches once a week, once a day? Who menstruate once a year? Who are constipated? Who can't wake up without a pill, sleep without a pill, have sex without a pill? Who can't celebrate without drugs? Is this health? If you can't control your temper, are you healthy? If you can't stop complaining, are you healthy?

In my book, my world, and according to nature, health is balance. If you go through your day with a runny nose, you are not healthy, you are sick. Only time will tell how sick. That we have grown accustomed to so many physical and mental imbalances, that we accept them as part of being alive, is a sad comment on how far our sense of well-being has been distorted. Will cancer some day become accepted as merely a part of growing older, such as arthritis, hardening of the arteries, glaucoma, etc. are now?

It is time for America to grow up. To give up its excessive ways, its degenerate dreams of world domination. The cancer that grows individually in the populace is the cause of the larger cancer that runs rampant through every segment of our government. The party's over. It is time to mediate. To retreat and rejuvenate and rediscover our lost way on the evolutionary path toward a Golden Age.

A book will never do it. People don't read books and then go out and make the kinds of changes in their lives that this book is about. Books are for people who aren't ready, who want to discuss it, argue about it, dabble in it. What this book is about *can't* be discussed, argued, dabbled in. It is much too far-reaching and dangerous for that.

Furthermore, the souls who have had the greatest effect on the people of this planet didn't write books, they spoke in parables, sayings, and mostly *lived the truth*. Jesus Christ, Buddha, Mohammed, Lao Tzu, Confucius. (L. Ron Hubbard wrote books, Dr. Moon writes books, Oral Roberts writes books, uses television, founds institutes of "higher learning.")

Were Jesus Christ living today, he wouldn't need television or a best-selling book. He would need only to live his life. The missionary ethic is practiced because the doctrines espoused are removed from truth. The Christian missionaries who thought they were bringing salvation to the savages of various lands brought, in fact, exactly the opposite: ruination. The examination of this tragedy goes far beyond the scope of my little book, but any consideration of the "salvation" the white man's missionaries brought to the American Indian shows it up for what it was . . . genocidal disaster.

The stupidity that considers "primitive" synonymous with "heathen" is ignorant beyond the need to discuss it. What the "primitive" Indian of North America did was live in accord with and as a part of the order of the universe. He had the spiritual maturity to *know* he was brother and sister to *all* living things under the sun. He knew that his health and happiness were dependent upon living in a constant state of gratitude for being *given* the opportunity to *be* a part of this infinitely large design.

The missionaries arrived on the scene to tell him different. That man and God were separate; that he must be baptized to be truly religious; that God passed "judgment" and demanded forgiveness; that to consider the buffalo as brother was beneath him. The white man, in two hundred short years, raped and destroyed North America's natural habitat beyond all recognition. The red man lived here for centuries without leaving a scar. We butchered the buffalo by the millions for the mere "sport" of it. When the red man killed, he used *every* part of the dead animal. We did it simply to watch them die, cut out their tongue or hang their beheaded trophies on our walls.

We brought them religion all right. Ours. We showed them how to commit crimes against nature so horrendous as to defy description and feel no remorse. And we *still* think we are going to avoid paying the tab. We *still* believe, in our Sunday-church-going arrogance, that we are separate from the laws that govern all other creatures on the face of the earth. We would do better to empty the zoos, plant corn and give thanks to the Sun God for a bountiful crop.

I don't expect, nor is it the motive of this book, to convert anyone to a lifetime of chewing grains. Those who will "get it" will do so by page one or simply by seeing the book sitting on a bookshelf. For the most part, it will come and go without a ripple. But if you are one of the few who recognize yourself in these pages, and if you survive and turn the corner toward instead of away from a larger life, try to remember the preceding few paragraphs. Don't try to ''save'' anyone. Let go of such arrogance. It will save you, time and again, from much anguish and frustration. And if you feel you have arrived, try to follow the *Kamikaze Cowboy Code:*

Chew your rice.

Drink your tea.

Wear your clothes.

And everything else will take care of itself.

If you think this sounds easy . . . try it for ten days. If you are successful, I will come cook for you for a year.

But notice that the Code does not include: Read your book. Watch your TV. Listen to your stereo. Talk to your psychiatrists, etc. Try it for ten days as you go about your normal daily routine. Remember: worrying, arguing, rationalizing are not allowed. Just chew, drink and wear!

And if, perchance, you should discover the *real* meaning of the Kamikaze Cowboy Code, then forget everything I have said. Do whatever you want. Eat, drink, wear whatever you want. You have arrived. Infinity is yours, is *you.* I'll come sit by your knee.